LETTERS TO MY YOUNGER SOUL

Published in the United Kingdom by
EIV Publishing Ltd,
admin@eivpublishing.com
www.eivpublishing.com

Cover design and layout :
Jodylynn Talevi of JT Design
jtalevi@gmail.com

ISBN 9798465915021

EIV PUBLISHING LTD

Dedication

This book is dedicated first to the 40+ women who wrote the letters. It should not be underestimated the hurdles that needed to be overcome to put your thoughts on paper. The hurdles were more challenging for some than for others but nevertheless, after this, it should never be said that you are not champions. Many started the journey with you and did not make it to the end, you absolutely rock!

Then, to all the women of the world. The ones who have cried, the ones who have laughed. The ones who are sad, and the ones who are happy. Those that loved and those that lost. Those who fought and lost and those who fought and won. Those that taught us wrong from right and loved us in all our mess. The women who struggled so that we don't have to. The ones who refused to be silent and the ones whose silence was louder than any voice. To all the women who have fallen but got up, and who showed up when they didn't need to or didn't want to.

To all the women of the world who make the world what it is.

CONTENTS

Introduction...6

Disclaimer..8

Be Who You Want To Be - Sharleen 'Red Fox'.....................9

Embrace The Totality Of Who You Are - Rozanna Wyatt........12

I Am Worthy - Dr Monique Y Wells..............................15

Strength In Mind And Body - Renata Pavrey.....................19

It Won't Last Forever - Keva....................................21

True Happiness - Monique Fierro.................................23

I Love You - Rose Calkins.......................................25

That Was Not You - Mariana Perri................................27

I Love You, I Forgive You and
I Thank you - Mir Scouten, BASc.................................30

You Got This - S...32

Turn Your Disappointments Into Triumphs -
Marigold Ndicho Katsande..35

I Am That Girl - Maxine Brown...................................40

Trust The Process - Ruby Rose Walker............................44

If Only You Knew - Tee Tee Sampson.............................47

Don't Just Survive, Thrive - Amanda Susan Grice................49

You Are Precious - Justina......................................52

Dear Future Entrepreneur - Charmaine............................55

You Are Beautiful - Rona Anderson..............................59

Be Confident - E.M Saheeb.......................................63

You Can Get Here From There - Jennifer Vitanzo.................65

This Too Shall Pass - Phoenix...................................69

You Are Treasure Not Trash - Tee Tee Sampson 75

It's Not Your Fault - J Clyne...................................78

Love Yourself - Maureen Weekes..82

Got Your Back Like A Rucksack - Leanne Burrowes...............................85

Hope After Heartbreak - Christina Morris...88

We Can Get Through This - Laura Smith 91

Listen To Silence -Meyrem Zekayi..95

We Are Free - Cynthia Butler Jackson..97

Be Bold, Be You - H.P..103

A Life Of Passion - Dr Yvonne Thompson 107

Pause, Breathe and Enjoy - Priscilla Muyunda.....................................109

Stay Strong - Rachel Delgado..112

You Will Never Lose Yourself - Amila Jašarević 114

Just The Way Your Supposed To Be - Natalie Joseph........................... 117

The Heart To Heart - J.L.B. 120

Trauma That Travels - Willelmina Joseph-Loewenthal 123

The Older You Get, The Better It Gets - Ruth Franks 127

Baten Down And Enjoy The Ride - Ingrid Collins..............................129

Don't Dilute You Attributes - Marigold Ndicho Katsande 131

Fear Not - Verona Ward..137

Know Your True Identity - Anita Barzey.................................141

What Is Your Why? - Denise Lorraine Aku Ledi.................................143

Real Change Starts Inside - Deeqa Ali 147

Your Talents Will Shine - Renata Pavrey..................................149

Dearest, Rarest, Unusual Me - Anointed Sonnet..............................151

Afterword 157

Introduction

There is a saying that there are two things for certain in life; death and taxes. If you don't know what that means, it is that whilst so much else in life is uncertain you can be sure you will die and you can be sure you will have to pay taxes, someway somehow.

But what is also certain is that there is nothing new under the sun when it comes to the human experience. If we've seen it once here then we'll have seen it somewhere else too. Technology may evolve and change but the human experience is something we all share and have a very similar experience of.

As a wife in the West, you might think in the East they have it worse, but do they? As a subjugated female in one part of the world, another's liberation looks attractive but what was the cost? The need to fully express ones self and be all you can be may have different parameters but is still a desire for everyone.

What about being single, having children earlier than expected or not in the way that it is expected? What about poor mental health, poor physical health and a lack of identity? All are third world problems as much as they are first albeit to different degrees.

No, some of us will never know hunger in the way that others have. We'll never know what it's like to walk bare foot for miles or to have no public health care, however the human condition; that of birth, growth, conflict, aspiration, emotion and mortality exists everywhere and it's that knowledge that started this book.

Deciding to share a letter to a younger self, was a seemingly simple undertaking for the women involved in collaborating in this book but it soon became a journey that some found difficult to take and could not complete. Those that did, had to overcome thoughts and feelings that they had long since buried and moved on from. Some found it a liberating experience, and whilst looking back realised just how far they had come.

No matter the experience, every letter was shared with love, every heart poured out what was in it, to not only heal themselves but to heal others. Every letter demonstrates a woman's affinity to her mothers, daughters, aunties, nieces, and grandchildren around the world.

Letters came from the land and the hearts of the likes of Brazil, The Bahamas, UK, USA, India, Sudan, Zimbabwe, France, The Netherlands, Australia, Jamaica and Canada.

The idea of sharing what we have learned is not new but it's a tradition that has served us all well. Learning from those that have gone before us, who have hindsight as a teacher and can help us to better navigate some of the challenges we may encounter, is now a profitable endeavour for some and for others it remains a campfire story, a slumber party heart-to-heart or a family pastime at grandma's knee.

Words are very powerful. They are damaging, at times toxic, impossible to take back once released and far reaching. Yet they are also redemptive, transformative, uplifting, soothing and life-giving.

So as you read each letter, may you find solace, strength, peace, encouragement, wisdom, passion, friendship, sisterhood, and freedom. May you remember you are not alone. May you cheer another woman on for making it through. May you realise that if she made it, you can too. May your distorted images be dashed and your hopes be restored, and may you be inspired to write your own...

Letter To YOUR Younger Soul.

Disclaimer

The views represented in this book are not representative of the views held by EIV Publishing, it's staff and or associates. All letters are published with the author's permission. These are their memories and thoughts, from their perspective, and they have tried to represent events as faithfully as possible.

Although this book is designed to provide accurate information in regard to the subject matter covered, the publisher and the authors assume no responsibility for errors, inaccuracies, omissions, or any other inconsistencies herein. This publication is meant as a source of inspiration for the reader, however it is not meant as a replacement for direct expert assistance. If such level of assistance is required, the services of a competent professional should be sought.

Be Who You Want To Be

Dear You,
    Dear Me,
        Dear, yes I'm talking to YOU!

What was the first thing you thought about when you woke up?

What was the first thing you did?

It's important to take a deep breath, stretch out your sleepy body with a reach to the sky and say to yourself:

'I AM ENOUGH, TODAY IS GOING TO BE AN AMAZING DAY'

Words I wished I knew back then when I was a younger you, a younger me, a younger human being, learning each day, growing each day, dealing with life each day…

Do not be afraid of each 'Test, Trail and Tribulation'
(The Triple T's) will only make you stronger even if you don't feel it at the time.

It's good to talk,
    It's good to read,
        It's good to write,
            It's good to get it out of your system.

It's never too late to be given advice and receive information, to help you grow and get by.

The choices we make, alter our future, but the paths we take can also change them. Nothing is set in stone if you feel you've made a few mistakes a few wrong turns, it's ok as long as you change the page, move on to the next, learn from the first page while creating new and positive pages.

Sometimes the key is just to be <u>Happy</u>, so I ask you now:

'WHAT MAKES YOU HAPPY?'

Well, more of that I say, enjoy life as life can be short, live life each day to the fullest don't let the little things get you down, as when you get older, when you're grown, when you're in a nice house working in your happy job and creating your own family all those pages that you turned, shaped you for today.

Remember to not hold anything in, speak to that friend, write in that book, take some me time out, write down your dreams and goals and work towards them.

Know you're Awesome and Amazing even if you don't feel it and others don't see it.

As you are special and that's what you need to KNOW!

KNOW IT
    FEEL IT
        LIVE IT!

Life doesn't have to be hard, our mind-set helps with decision making, you want to be happy, strong, motivated, loved and so much more.

That's when the Triple T's come along… take a long DEEP breath and then face it like a bull charged with positivity, come out the other side strong more educated, but HAPPY!

That word comes up a lot, Happy!
But it's important to be happy, your emotions and your insides,

Need Happy,
     Need love,
          Need laughter,

So that you can stay well from the inside out, giving yourself great emotions to make positive decisions, to stay happy, this will help towards your everyday life decisions.

Everyone learns different,
          Thinks different,
               Lives different,

You're amazing don't watch that, don't compare, remember

Who you are,
     What your goals are,
          What you want to achieve.

BE WHO YOU WANT TO BE.

But if you don't know yet just,

BE YOU.

Yours Sincerely,

You,
ME…

Sharleen a.k.a Red Fox

Embrace The Totality Of Who You Are

Dear Younger Self,

It's time to embrace the totality of who you are so you can become unstoppable.

It took me forty-one years to understand this and to surrender to the truest notion of what success means – to embrace the totality of who you are.

You see, I had spent so many years achieving in action by obtaining fancy degrees, ticking boxes, and hitting milestones like six-figure salaries. These were societal standards of success, after all. And yet, while I was grateful for all I had achieved, I knew success extended beyond this, at least it did for me.

My soul deeply desired more. It was curious, ready to be courageous, and eager to shine brightly. It wanted to experience life and success as it had never done before. My higher-self wanted to break free. Breaking free meant totally accepting me.

It was time to stop downplaying my strengths, minimising my goals, and abiding by what I now call "good girl syndrome." It was time to overcome my fear of rejection. I no longer wanted to play it 'safe' because I knew I was not experiencing life as my truest-highest-self.

I was unconsciously self-sabotaging myself from embracing the totality of who I was and who I could be. Inward action in the form of inner work was needed. This was the only way to get to the root of what was holding me back.

The inner work I pursued was like walking into a sticky cobweb in the middle of the night. Where you don't know how long it will take to break free, but you know, you will break free.

This journey was the biggest variable in moving the needle on my success. It allowed me to release everything that previously kept me stuck and from proudly integrating every strength and talent that makes me, me.

I realised success is an emotional process. Inner acceptance is far more important than outer achievement because no outer achievement will ever be enough if inner acceptance is not present. This isn't to take away from all those great accomplishments you've achieved. Be proud of them because I know what it took to get there!! I'm simply bringing awareness to the truth I wish I had known.

Stepping into your greatness as a person means letting go. Letting go of the mask, the veil of shame, and the negative thoughts in your mind because these are what hold you back from all that you are and all that you can be.

And so, the greatest marker of success is when the real you is unveiled, allowing you to live with purpose, grace, and ease. Inner acceptance is abundant and free, and as a result, your life and external success will feel complete.

May today be the day that you step into your greatness and embrace the totality of who you are and who you can be. Let curiosity and courage be your guiding posts as you embark on this journey. With compassion and a gentle open heart, I ask you, "What do you need to embrace and/or let go of so you can embrace the totality of who you were always meant to be?"

When you discover this, you will be unstoppable and free, designing your life and success as you had always dreamed.

With love,

Rozanna Wyatt

I Am Worthy

Dear Younger Self,

I've reached the 60-year milestone of life and I must say that the road to get here has been nothing less than an obstacle course.

Even the good times have been peppered with obstacles ...

... almost every step of the way.

This may sound harsh, I know.

But I don't want you to think I'm bitter! I am tremendously blessed and have always been so.

What I want you to know is that the key to having a wonderful life is deciding how you view the obstacles you encounter.

If you view them as gifts – even blessings – then you'll experience life with an abundance of grace and ease!

If you view them as curses, you will invite more of them into your environment, and you will descend into a downward spiral that will eventually make your life miserable.

When I look at the "smooth" parts of my road, I think about how hard

I worked to achieve the things I felt were important – from taking drum lessons at Texas Southern University to bring some soul into the Carmel Cadette drum corps in high school, to giving up three days of travel abroad with my sorority sisters to study for my veterinary pathology boards (which I passed on the first try).

I also think about how I viewed my accomplishments as being significant because I was able to go from "Point A to Point B," taking the direct route from idea to achievement in the shortest amount of time possible.

No meandering. No indecision. I was a woman on a mission, and I was in control of my life.

That was an integral part of the pride I felt in my achievements.

When I look back now, I see that the road to these successes was incredibly rough.

But the achievements themselves were big enough and satisfying enough to dull the memories of the obstacles associated with accomplishing them.

I think about how happy I was to achieve these things, and I realise that my happiness was fleeting. It only lasted a few hours to a few days, and then I turned my gaze toward the next thing to be achieved.

Happiness feels great, but it is not the same as joy. It stems from external experiences and is an expression of your reaction to them.

Joy comes from within. It can be harder to achieve, but it is more sustainable when it is achieved. It is a conscious choice and therefore, it is something you always have available to you.

I strongly encourage you to always CHOOSE JOY!

When I look at what I remember as the rough parts of my road, I can divide them into two categories. Some of the difficult times were due to EXTERNAL challenges.

Something completely beyond my control happened and I was prevented from doing something I wanted to do.

Or someone I trusted betrayed me.

In these cases, I think about how I dug deep into myself to find the determination to move on. I think about the need to forgive the person who betrayed me to move on.

To do these things, I needed a strong sense of self, and more importantly, a strong sense of self-worth.

Other rough times were due to INTERNAL challenges. I wasn't seeking or dealing with something outside myself. I was struggling to find or accept something within myself.

Maybe I did something I knew was wrong, failed at something I felt I should have been able to achieve, or pretended to be something I was not.

"How could I have done that?" I'd repeatedly ask myself. "Why did I do it?"

During these times, I wasn't exactly sure who I was in those moments – days – weeks – compared to who I believed I wanted to be.

Whether the source of my discomfort was internal or external, I was impatient. I wanted the pain, disappointment, uncertainty, self-doubt, and fear to be gone IN THAT MOMENT.

I wanted to leap over these feelings instead of embracing them, examining them, working through them.

I wanted to ignore my inner guidance. I didn't want to accept the truth that the core of my being was offering for me to see, to use to my best advantage …

… the truth that I AM ENOUGH.

I AM WORTHY.

Finally, I learned that wilfully ignoring this guidance, rejecting this truth, only prolonged my discomfort. I learned the power and the necessity of self-esteem and self-forgiveness.

And I learned that you cannot forgive yourself without self-love.

Younger Self, the most important thing you can do in life is love yourself.

Love yourself as the imperfectly perfect person that God created you to be.

Because God – the Universe – whatever higher being you believe in – is in you. And that's what makes you ENOUGH.

Love always,

Monique

Strength In Mind And Body

Dear Younger Self,

You haven't seen much of life, but even a decade or more can feel like a lifetime when you've spent all of it as a misfit. Born underweight, diagnosed with childhood asthma, and living your infancy more in hospitals than at home, you've been made to believe that you're not strong enough.

You might be excluded from school games and discouraged from childhood sports, but never let others decide what you can or cannot do. The doctors might advise, parents mean well, teachers are cautious — they fear for what might happen, and instead cripple you with their worries.

Your family and society are around you, but they do not live inside your body. And only you know what your body is capable of. They might call your muscles weak, dismiss your poorly functioning lungs, declare that you can't run or skip or cycle or play tennis because you're not medically fit. Don't let their idea of physical activity decide what your body knows it can do.

Like a science fiction movie, I travel through these words from your future. I'm here to report that your older self has not only run several marathon races, but has also trained in martial arts like Muay Thai, Karate and Capoeira, and performed dance on stage — overcoming asthma and many other obstacles along the way.

Find joy in the little things, whether climbing the stairs to your favourite bookshop, or taking the dog for a walk. All that's needed is one small step that ultimately leads to larger strides.

It might not seem like much now, but every tiny initiative only opens up new avenues of belief for all the things you can accomplish. One foot in front of the other, and before you know it you complete a marathon. Life can be a marathon, too. It takes a long time to get through it all, with several defeats and losses along the way. But you ultimately do reach the finish line, whether you crawl through it or jump over it.

Your body can overcome anything, if you set your mind to it. People will try to pull you down, bring up your past and say you won't be able to do something; tell you your body isn't up for it—that you'll injure yourself, or collapse, or die. Yes, they're even willing to see you dead rather than believing that you can actually achieve something!

Your body is yours alone, and only your organs, bones, muscles, tissues and nerves know what they can and cannot do. Others can guide you, but they cannot be you.

Muscle soreness, dehydration, lungs filled with breath, a heart filled with joy, achy feet, a flexible spine—let your body be the one to decide for you, and listen to it. No matter what today looks like, believe in your tomorrow. Eat well, exercise regularly, think positive thoughts, breathe deeply, stretch, soak in the sunshine, and live with passion. Nurture your mind, body and spirit because they will carry you through when no one else is around.

Renata Pavrey

It Won't Last Forever

Keva,

I come to you in good cheer, truth, and divinity. I am writing to help pave the way for your mind to develop good habits. Decisions you make now, will lead you to develop good patterns or procrastinate on developing good patterns. The level of endurance and patience to make good decision and act justly is a reoccurring application. Therefore, the path to progressing good nurturing habits is simple. Trial failure with increasing effort and feel pain to gain.

Put together learned lessons from your past and apply them to the new lessons you learn today. Not every day is peachy and glamorous, but you have managed to manoeuvre through life thus far. The epiphany of living a happy, healthy, and wealthy lifestyle is to do it your way. Learn now to be content with every outcome good or bad. Be respectful of your elder's and spend a lot of time with them. Their continuous effort to wake up daily and live, will give you courage to carry on.

Developing your unique and authentic self will take time. As you go through these next phases in your journey, keep in mind that love for thyself is most vital to the level of progression you will achieve.

Persistence and a not giving up attitude will be full force in the years to come so get your mind and body in shape now. In the midst of coping with daily living, I need you to jot down these experiences, devastations, heartaches, headaches, and disappointments.

Devastations are directions into your destiny. Designed to detour you from all the wonderful successful destinations. Mark each of life's widespread devastations as a shocking feeling that will ultimately be uplifting. God will replace burdens with blessings in due season. Disappointments are tribulations that have numerous trails. Verily, it will be a good verdict but chose to face everything and rise. Do not neglect priorities and opportunities. Be wise to accept opportunities, be relentless to succeed and rise to the occasion. Every time you overcome a challenge God prepares another disappointment to show your humanity. Remind yourself that you are braver than you believe, stronger than you feel, and fearless of anything or anyone. God will grant you the desires of your heart once you do what is right and just.

Heartaches are heartfelt moments that create love and virtue. It will happen often, and everyone will offer love, but it can only be genuine to the extent of what you perceive as true. Until time tells the tale, you must believe the best in that person. No heartaches last long unless it is held on to. Be tenderhearted and free to love as you would love yourself. For all the headaches take a pill, Literally! Aspirin, Tylenol, or what ever headache medicine that is useful and harmless, USE IT!

Stay away from the drugs that cause more than you bargain for. Narcotics and Alcohol are instant remedies that satisfy the moment, but they can lead to a bad habit. The headache will turn into anxiety and you will lose a lot of valuable time chasing a cure to end a bad habit. Take a chill pill and relax.

Rely on God's understanding and your abilities to make good decisions. Decide today to become intune with God's voice and follow your intuition. With you and God, everything is possible. Believe in what you want to achieve and earn the win!

Keva

True Happiness

Are you happy? Most people say "yes" without thinking. That's what I used to do. And I was for the most part. I had a man I loved and two beautiful girls that have kept life fun but I wasn't happy personally. I had put expectations on my life that were unattainable. Perfection. Passions. Career. All while still being a stay at home wife and mother. Even though I was never taught to, I felt the need to have my life completely mapped out at a young age. But that's not how life really works, is it?

The truth is that I am thirty-four years old and I am just now figuring my life out. At least, that's how it feels. I always had it in my head that I needed to be a stay at home mom after pursuing my career for a while. That is what I was 'made to do'. In reality, even though I enjoyed being a stay at home mom, I wasn't fulfilled by it and it became overwhelming and isolating. I felt intense guilt that I wanted a change because I wasn't sure what that change was. For some reason, I grew up thinking that you are who you are and you don't change. Once you choose something that's it. But people do change and it's normal. It's called growth.

This may seem like a "duh" statement but it was something that was never explained to me. I had to figure it out the hard way. Now I know that change is a good thing. After some health issues, I was forced to make some changes to my lifestyle. I sent my girls to daycare and school and gave myself time to rest and heal physically. During that time I also reignited my passions and now have an idea of what I want to do. By giving myself time to pursue my passions, I have truly become happy in all aspects of my life.

What I want from life will most likely change in the future. Different phases bring new challenges and ways of life. I don't have everything figured out and I don't need to. I take it day by day. Most importantly, I do my best to stay true to what makes me happy, not what is socially acceptable. I think as we grow up we see the paths other people take and it somehow gets ingrained in us that we need to strive for the same goals. Go to college, graduate, get married, buy a house and start having kids. As I've gotten older, I have seen first hand that that may not be what is best for your life even if it is what is expected.

Even though I have children I can also look back at my life and see I would have been fine not having them. It's a hard thing to admit because I truly love them, but there are times that I wonder what life would have been like without them. Your life can go so many different ways. Why limit it to what others have chosen for you?

So are you truly happy? Or are you giving an automated response? If you realise you aren't happy, what do you need to do to change that? Give yourself permission to find out what will make you happy and feel fulfilled. Have fun, reinvent yourself. Life is too short to feel stuck or unhappy. Don't wait. Just start.

Monique Fierro

I Love You

Dear Rosemary,

I love you. Take good care of yourself. You are very precious and beautiful. You make this world a lovely place. Keep on shining your light and using and sharpening your gifts and talents and sharing them with loving lifelong beautiful friendships.

Please know that you are very smart, and have a great capacity to love, learn, and grow. Share it! You are strong, wise, and very capable. You are wanted, respected, loved, desired, and favoured.

Rest and nourish yourself. Stay close to God and rest in His love and seek his guidance.

Jesus loves you. Your body is a gift. Love it and care for it. Also, welcome true and honourable affection.

Take courage and step forward to learn new skills, create new ideas, invent new things, build new things. Be happy to be alive. Take the time you need. Be kind to yourself. Enjoy the beauty of creation. Be present in the moment.

Dance, sing, create art...do what you enjoy.

Forgive yourself and others. Rest in the fact that you are a miracle and created for such a time as this. You are worthy of being treated with great love, respect, kindness, and generosity.

Please travel the world in great health, with love, kindness, peace, and joy. Love your family and let them love you!

I love you Rosemary. You are adorable.

Rose Calkins

That Was Not You

Dear Me,

It may seem strange but I will start my letter telling you that you must let go of your prejudice about mental health. Try to understand that asking for professional help may be the healthiest choice you can make for your future.

I ask you to stop and think of the many times you felt so angry that you blurted out awful offences to those who love you the most. Try to remember how the words just flew out of your mouth without filters, even if they were not what you thought was true. Try to remember the heavy weight on your shoulders every time you broke something or slammed a door so hard that chips of paint would fall off the door frame. That was not really you!

You are sweet, you are caring. You are not that horrible person who, at the first sign of frustration, set off to hurt anyone on your way, and, most of all, yourself.

Take a deep breath and let the sleepless nights you dove into useless tasks you could not bring yourself to stop sink in. That was not you being creative, that was not you.

Reflect on the sadness you felt when something was missing inside you. Remember why you sought alcohol and random drugs.

Remember how you tried to fill that void with sex, believing every man that crossed your path to be your knight in shining armour. That was not you!

Accept it when someone suggests you make an appointment with a psychologist and don't get offended when your mother suggests you have your brain scanned. She is right, her instincts are working. You need that help.

Someday up ahead, you'll look back and realise you missed so many chances in life because you could not focus on a task long enough to see it through. You'll notice that much of that void could have been filled with moments of sheer enjoyment of life, instead of this unnerving feeling that you are on the wrong path. You'll come to figure out you spent most of your life running away from something that was inside you.

Let me give it to you straight up: You are bipolar!

If you don't keep telling yourself that mental illness is a sign of weakness, and if you don't keep on rejecting the idea that you do have real issues that will not go away without help, you might just be able to find your inner peace sooner. You might be able to see your dreams through.

And, most importantly, there will come a day when you become a mother and you will look at your young daughter and see that she, just like you, is suffering the same ills you did, but with a lot more intensity. And you might be able to help her before she is so desperate that she believes taking her life is the only way out of this void.

You might also avoid regretting the many times you yelled at her so hard that she shied away from you, scared. You might even feel less guilty for having overreacted to a small child being a small child.

I beg of you, don't push it off to the future, look for help. I promise you that looking for help is an act of courage and that it will help you find your way through this jungle, called life, with a lot more serenity.

Be well, my dear me, and take care.

Me

Mariana Perri

I Love You, I Forgive You and I Thank you

Dear Mir,

I'm your older self and I want to tell you not to worry about your career. Just follow your passions and you'll get where you want to be. Right now you just finished University and there is a financial crisis. You will find a job soon enough, just remember to always be honest. When you do the right thing, even if it seems hard, there's always a reward. Being honest means being true to yourself as well as to others. Right now you live in The Netherlands and you studied for six years, but you never stopped following your passions: connecting people, writing stories and healing people. Even though you were born in The Netherlands, and you will make an international career because you are fluent in four languages, the only thing you need to do is follow your passions and stay focused, always keep that in mind.

Now it is ten years later and I'm writing you another letter. Remember when your boss was making love to his mistress on his desk and you caught them in the act? You got fired the next day, but if he had not done so, you wouldn't have gotten that job in the French speaking part of Belgium. Remember that you were honest and told the HR manager that it was that one woman on the team who was not honest to the other women? She got fired and the team was doing a much better job after that. There's always a reward for being honest.

Now it is twenty years later and I'm writing you another letter.

Remember when your Radiation free B&B was doing great? That is because you followed your passion to connect people and you received electro hypersensitive guests from all over the world. Remember when your Radiation free B&B was closed because of your divorce? That gave you the opportunity to start healing more people remote by giving them Shamballah Multi-Dimensional Healing. Even though you lost nine babies, everything did turn out fine. Being divorced and having to raise a child with the man you don't want to see anymore would have been terrible. There's always a higher purpose if something bad happens to you, just follow your passions and trust that the universe knows what is best for you.

Now it is thirty years later and I'm writing you another letter. Remember when your career finally started going where you wanted it to be twenty years ago? You would not have been as wise as you are now and PR/HR consultancy is involving a lot of wisdom and people knowledge. It is also involving a lot of writing and you love your work! Now you even have time for writing in your spare time and you're writing a book on how to grow a business stress free with PR! You found the love of your life and you are living with him in a house with a garden. All you created and put in the cosmos for your perfect future came true. You are still healing people and connecting people via LinkedIn, so you followed all your passions! You started The Soft Revolution Of Love #SoftRevolutionOfLove, which is trending on Twitter! You wrote a children's book and even translated it from Dutch to English yourself! Don't worry about getting them published, keep following your passions, stay honest and true to yourself and all will be well Mir.

I love you, I forgive you, I thank you Mir.

Love, Mir Schouten, BASc from your soul.

You Got This

Dear S,

I write this not to scare or deter you, but to spur you on and maybe change some things along the way. You're passionate (hotheaded?) And when hurt, you're all talk. But you're a doer. You are resilient. You are kind and you are grateful. You are a mom! And a wife and daughter and sister. You experience heartache and hurt, bad relationships and abuse. Yes, you read that right. Abuse. Your passion sometimes gets the best of you. And in college it will do just that. You'll allow that passion to take over. It will overpower the warning bells screaming in your head. You will not be permanently bruised, but your heart will hurt, and your head will be muddled. You will pull through, though. You always do.

Some will say your passion is a cry for attention. Maybe. But from my viewpoint it is what makes you *you*. You cry at the drop of a hat. You feel deeply when children are hurt, when bad things happen to good people. Your first inclination is to help. I don't want to discourage that. It's a great quality. But trust your gut more. You should help people, if they want it. Ask first. Or let them come to you. And if your gut tells you it's not a good idea… listen to it. Not to be mean or blow someone off. But that gut feeling is always right. It will save you a job, a friendship, much sadness.

And don't worry about your tears! It won't be until you're over 40 that you won't care so much. You won't. It's ok to cry - when you're happy, when you're scared, when you're sad or mad. Shrug it off sooner. It's not a plea for attention. It's your body's reaction to things.

Start yoga now. It will keep you limber and in shape. It will help with the tears, and maybe keep away the knot that forms in your chest.

Your dad tells you that what doesn't kill you makes you stronger. He's right. You always come out on the other side.

Now that I've scared you, I want you to know that your life is good - despite the bad stuff. You have two beautiful children - one boy and one girl (just like you said you would in 5th grade!) You don't teach math, though. However, you are a teacher. A mother, a friend. A wife, a helper. You are enough. It takes time, tears, and years to realise that.

I know it's hard. Believe me. Telling yourself you are enough. It's hard work. Don't listen to your sister when she calls you fat. You'll grow out of the weight by high school.

You're smart. You're kind. You'll face challenges when you move to Dallastown. Get explicit directions to Tracey's birthday party. It might mean making friends sooner. Being accepted sooner.

Always keep your grace and your smarts and your "goody-two-shoes" demeanour. Be the good Samaritan. You'll save the life of a college acquaintance. You'll help a boy who breaks his arm in a fall off his bike. You'll let his mom know where he is and that he's ok. Possibly just as important, you'll show your children how to do these things, too.

Go down south to college. Stay away from a particular boy (actually a man) because he will hurt you. Stay focused. Enjoy Spain. Pay off the credit card. Take the higher paying job. It's ok. You'll realise your dreams and then your dreams will change. That's ok. Don't despair. You will persevere.

When the wedding finally comes, listen to your gut. Pare down on the guest list, the food, the DJ. But don't use more credit. It will create tension. That tension will last well into your marriage. It won't be let go.

Stick up for yourself. Be strong. Don't let anyone bring you down. Don't lose yourself. It's so hard, but you can do it.

You are kind and caring. You give up your career so you can raise your children. You want them to know you and love you. You want to be there for them. And you will. But ask for help when you need it. Motherhood can be overwhelming. But you got this! Show your kids how to ask for help.

As I write this, the whole world is the midst of a pandemic. What does this mean? People are getting deathly ill. The virus doing this is extremely contagious. You will have to stay home for months on end. School will be taught remotely. Your kids will be anxious. You will be anxious. Your husband will worry about business. But you all come out on the other side.

There's still remote learning, but it will eventually get back to normal. Do your part to slow the spread. Wear the mask. Limit contact with store employees and people you don't know. It's hard. And it's scary. But you got this!

Your husband's business will recover. Your kids will get used to the new school routine. You will find your groove. Lean into it. Don't run away from it. Be cautious, but don't be afraid.

You are an amazing woman. You help your children navigate remote learning. You help your mother-in-law. You keep a neat house. You help your friends when you can. You help women better themselves. You offer support to so many. You got this!

And, finally, I know you know this, but always choose kindness. It matters. Even in the face of adversity. You got this!

'S'

Turn Your Disappointments Into Triumphs

My Dear Younger Self,

Some do it out of malice, some out of ignorance and others who may have suffered the same fate at the hands of others inflict emotional harm on others, seemingly oblivious to the possible consequences of their vindictive actions on their undeserving innocent victims. Yes, people can and will disappoint you my dear.

That is how unfair life can be.

While you view the world through innocent eyes, trusting and believing most of what you see, hear and are promised, the world has some surprises for you my dear, good ones and bad ones, some of them downright nasty which can be a shock to your system.

These disappointments may leave you angry, mostly at yourself, wondering if and why you have been so naive and gullible, blind to the deceitful behaviour of those you trust, even with your heart. You may feel so hurt you may decide it is perhaps better to never open your heart again. Who can blame you?

Self-preservation is only a natural reaction in us humans.

My dear Younger Self I want to urge you to dare to be vulnerable and learn to trust again. It is not a sin to trust. It is only a sin to allow past hurts to completely close the door to future happiness.

Wallowing in self-pity can easily blinker you and result in a distorted view of the world that will make you believe that you are okay but them and the whole world suck.

Understanding and forgiveness will free your aching heart. Lean on your Creator for strength and guidance.

You can transform your thinking to the more liberating view that you are ok and them and the world are also okay. Remember that even you too are not perfect.

Only God is perfect. No human being can ever be perfect.

By all means:

Don't		Dwell	
Inconsolable	and	Incapacitated	by
Sadness,		Sorrow	and self-pity
Accepting	and	Allowing	
Pompous,		Parasitic	people,
Proud	with	Poverty	of
Openness	and	Obligation,	
Inhumane	and	Incapable	of
Natural		Nurturing,	
Troublesome	and	Truth-less,	

Mean	and	Mindless,		
Exploitative	and	Egotistical,		
Nonsensical	and	Never	capable	of
Trustworthiness	nor	Thankfulness		
Selfish	and full of	S..t		

Staying with such people can potentially:

Destroy

Incapacitate

Stress

Aggravate

Punish

Perish

Overpower

Impact

Negate

Torment

Molest

Exterminate

Nullify

Terrify and

Suffocate you!

Instead, my dear Younger Self, I would like to pass on this wisdom:

Smile and love again. Yes, you can do it! Go on!

Survive

Move on

Innovate

Laugh

Energize

And also my dear Younger Self:

Learn

Overcome

Volunteer

Explore

Accomplish

Grow

Aspire

Inspire

Nurture yourself and others.

That, my dear Younger Self is called survival.

With much love

Your Older Self

Marigold Ndicho Katsande

I Am That Girl

Letter to little Maxine,

you survived and overcame because Greater is He that is in you, than he that is in the World - 1 John 4:4

You were left broken in pieces. With a foundation like yours, it would prove impossible to stand.

No roots neither identity, but yet you still smile on some days. But on other days you were in too much despair to see ...any good.

I saw me through crippled Broken Lenses that meant I overlooked you.

But yet you refuse to break because there is a deeper truth so powerful that dwells in you. It's Called Divine Power and destroys rays of darkness.

Maxine, you are me and I am you, as my recovery yields and reveals more, the authentic me appears, and so you are being revealed more into reality, more alive.

A layer of the false maladaptive self-disperses. It has been such a painful and yet powerful journey, all life offered you was disappointment and failures; dissatisfaction, rejection, abandonment, and utter obliteration of self, but you are still here!

Your tears were so heavy and weighty, and you never understood why, so you came to the conclusion that is simply this… it is what always happens to me. Domestic Violence, I was used to it; a programmed victim.

A victim, try as I may, nothing good ever happens to me…but I've come to tell you the curse is broken.

I am the adult part of you. I hear chains breaking and bondage fleeing. I hear, and I boast of the greatness of God.

The trauma started when you came in the World, your mother gave you to them, she never looked back, and never cared; her character ruthless to the core.

I survived I still smile because I overcame evil with good, Mum. I don't know if I love you because I never knew you. But I see you when I look in the mirror. Peace to you, I am over it.

You, Little Maxine, were left with trauma and repression. It had its own will, it explains our inconsistency and lack of stability, paralysed by fear and not knowing how to be and no sense of belonging, we wore our shame. Everyone ridiculed, but they are not laughing now!

Utter confusion, nothing but fragments left to be impacted. You always settled for less and you gave more than you ever took, always losing out. But I thank God for Salvation and favour and thank God for being a shield and a protector to me.

You needed healing but all I did was give you Crack Cocaine and Alcohol. I, the adult, made those choices, and I became another weapon against you. I should have been stronger, I should have been braver, but they never gave me self-worth.

Will you ever understand, I was powerless then, but I am committed to you. I am 11 years clean and I come to whisper my hello to you.

To let you know that it is not over, the dreams can still appear, that is our work. I am stronger, little Maxine and so much wiser...lets re-educate, let's build it has been too long. Those areas where we thought were too far gone, it's only a mindset ruled by fear. I watched Joyce Meyer and got my mind renewed. The Scriptures and verses made me aware and the Salvation Plan made me whole.

Those voices don't scare me no more, fear does not bound me no more, I left the House, but the house was in me I was trapped and stuck. Demons were on my heels.

They said we could not be anybody... but whose report do you believe? You have been through so much and that is what we use, we use the pain as a testimony. Because someone needs to know they can survive; the aftermath, the severity of Cruelty. Cruelty, you're not that big and bad now... I am a wearing the boxing gloves.

Did you have a dream? No, it was never safe; our identity is lost in the past. I speak power by saying your identity is you. It's in your greatness, the price was paid to be a part of a bigger story, eventually to be revealed.

I pray inner peace, real peace remember that you are unique and one of a kind, born in a complex complication. They said you are uneducated and untrained and unskilled but yet God says 'you wait and see.'

I salute you. I celebrate you for the ability of overcoming, always remembering God's love and truth that stands the test of time, unbreakable, unshakeable...

The Potters House is where I am, and God is bringing me out Pure Gold.

My faith in Jesus brings me into my life. It has elevated me and restored the areas of damage, your name is Victory.

God never makes a mistake. I found God to be a Father, the nurturing and love and long-suffering coaxing me out gently. I was so stubborn, but I yielded. The best decision was to trust the process we are living each day.

I love you God, I could write about your great love forever, my heart has a home now we are one…you can trust me.

I am that Girl

Touched by The Creative Creator, it's Supernatural

Maxine Brown

Trust The Process

To my darling Ruby Rose,

I know you feel alone in this world. I know you're confused, anxious, and feel unheard. You feel very deeply, you'll learn all about that someday. You'll learn about your true self, your identity, and your purpose, and you will be able to make much more sense of the world.

People have hurt you profoundly, and you've got a few more of those to come I'm afraid. But know that it's not because you're not enough, it's because they've not yet learnt to love themselves.

This is their journey and burden to carry, so be kind to yourself and let this go. You're wiser than your years, people can't always understand you or respect you as much as you deserve, this can be hard but I hope that me telling you this helps you get through some of the tough times. Keep living true to yourself. You're exactly where you're supposed to be.

The world has not passed you by, everything that is happening is right on course so that you can learn who you truly are and serve your purpose. You're stronger than you know, and people need your light.

I know you're frustrated, I heard you ask 'Is this it?'

'Absolutely not!' I can't wait for you to get over to this side of time, to wake up to who you truly are and start to understand the universe and that you're part of something much greater.

It's been a rough ride, and there's a few more big bumps in the road, but I promise you it gets great! The world is a powerful place, beyond the stressful job that keeps you up at night, the people around you, your body image, college degrees and material things.

It's all right here, waiting for you.

You will go on to help people and you will live a life in line with who you truly are. You'll help people live their purpose and have an impact on the world. Hang in there Rubes, you're EXACTLY where you're supposed to be.

So now, a couple of pieces of advice from your future self and this state of mind to help you along the way. I know you're stubborn, but trust me on these:

- Be kind to yourself. You are far too harsh and you have so much to be proud of.

- It's OK to ask for help. You can't do everything alone.

- Trust your intuition, when things don't feel right, walk away.

- Don't take everything so seriously! Have fun, lighten up!

- Perfectionism is not helping you. There's no such thing as perfect. Let that shit go!

- Meditate. I know you think that you can't do it, but you can. It's going to change your life.

- Don't settle for things or people in your life that don't light you up.

- Manifesting works! Get experimenting with that one.

So my dear one, I'll leave you with this: You are perfect just the way you are, you should be so so proud of how far you've come and who you are as a person.

Trust the process, it's all here waiting for you.

The future is bright and you have so much to give.

I love you in every moment, I'm with you each step of the way.

All my love, with all my heart,

Ruby Rose

If Only You Knew

Dear Natasha,

If only you could see the beauty within you, how perfectly crafted your body is, and how amazingly gifted your mind. Despite what others may say, your size 14 frame is beauty personified, as will your size 18, 20, and 22 to come. Don't be scared, you'll carry each stone like precious jewels, as they've brought you three amazing children and an angel baby too.

I need you to know that your beauty never changes. I wish I could reach back and pull you forward into the time you can look into the mirror and feel the perfect peace that you'll later learn to experience. It's real, and it's yours for the taking! Your present and past will have little hold over you, once you come to the realisation of who you are in Christ. A child of the most high God.

I know you're carrying generations of hurt, and emotions that run deep. So, when a man tells you that you are 'too big', 'not attractive enough', 'not the quintessential sexy', fear not, they really don't know what they are talking about. It's the insecurity within you that leaves you believing what you hear, not the fact that they are right, or even worthy to be listened too. Fear that you constantly battle, as you refuse to allow it to take the lead. Keep it up! Soon you will learn to silence fear, and remind it that it is your slave and never your master. Soon you'll have your very own chocolate King who loves every curve you have.

Don't be discouraged, fear may never leave entirely, but you'll learn to harness it. Your sadness will become the fuel to keep you moving forward until you find your flow. Rest when you must, but get back up! Don't fill guilty for the times you rest. Rest isn't a weakness, it's a strength. Learn it quick girl! As one of your greatest struggles is to say 'no'. Your day off, isn't you 'doing nothing' when someone asks for assistance. It's you recuperating, so that you're never giving out of an empty vessel.

By the time you reach 2002 you'll be rid of that dysfunctional relationship you've been bound in. You'll have several years of trying to find love. Until you eventually learn that love starts from within you. And after all that searching, you'll end up marrying that same young man you discarded circa 1993! Imagine him minus that hideous jerry curl, a bald head, and filled out a bit, and you'll begin to see what you failed to all those years ago. Trust me, his chocolate skin is just as scrumptious as you've always thought, and now it's all yours!

Together you make a couple to be reckoned with. You'll have some ups and downs, but it's all worthwhile. Because in his eyes you'll see your truest self, your beauty and your worth. Not because it comes from him, but because together you will tear down those years of lies the world told you, and receive the grace and truth of your heavenly creator.

Tee Tee Sampson

Don't Just Survive, Thrive

There will be times where it may feel like you have no choice in the matter, that you have no power or control over your life, or that there is no way to make it out of your situation alive; but I'm here to assure you that you do have a choice, you will regain control, and that you will make it out not only alive, but stronger still for it. There will be multiple times in your life that you feel this way, and each time you do you will have to remind yourself that there is light in the midst of your darkest hours.

When you are diagnosed Bipolar I at age 25 believe the doctor. Don't fight the diagnosis. By fighting the diagnosis, you are only putting off the inevitable, and you are only making your situation worse. You are not buying time. Listen to the professionals instead of taking it upon yourself to say that they are wrong, you are right, and therefore, you won't return to them for follow-up visits or take the drugs they prescribe.

From the very first time you hear the diagnosis, go home, tell your husband, and begin including him in all psychiatrists and some therapist visits so that he can begin to understand the disease too. Because maybe, just maybe, if he learns about it early enough in your diagnosis he will see it as the same thing as a cancerous tumour – just on your brain. Give him an ultimatum early on. Tell him that either he comes along with you to learn about the disease, so that he can be supportive and understand the lifelong consequences of the diagnosis or walk away early in the marriage. Do not stick around hoping for something to change. Bipolar I is not curable, does not go into remission, and even when medicated and functioning at a high level there is always the reality that at any given moment the fragile ecosystem you have created through medication therapy, talk therapy, and other support could break, taking you back to square one. And if your husband is not willing to love, support, and help you inevitably cycle through, then save yourself the time, energy, and heartbreak of sticking by him.

When, at 25, you first see the words Bipolar I begin searching for a psychiatrist you can trust, as well as a therapist you can't outsmart. Don't settle for the first ones that you come across or that have appointments open. Find a Care Team you can work with because ultimately, they are, as the name suggests, your team. And every time you move to a new location go through it again. Interviewing the doctors and therapists just as they interview you. You will come to learn that trust is the key to not only surviving, but thriving when you have Bipolar I.

While you are going to want to blame a lot of things on being Bipolar I, your mom's death when you were five (5); your brother's suicide when you were eighteen (18); or your grandmother, who was also your best friend's death at eighteen (18) you are going to have to own up to choices you make without using these as crutches. Poor decisions are poor decisions. You've never been declared incompetent, except for that week you spent in the psych ward, and therefore you were technically of sound mind when you made each of your mistakes. Own them. No excuses. You did that. Even if it doesn't feel good in the morning light, you made the choice, so embrace the experience, learn from the mistake, and live with little regret because you did what you came into this world to do.

You don't have to apologise for being you. You are you – a unique human being that is unlike anyone else. You are going to have friends that come in and out of your life. You are going to have friends that you thought you'd have forever leave your life. Do not beat yourself up and let the voice in your head convince you it is because you are a toxic person that these people are no longer your friends. Forgive them instead. And then move on.

Be willing to meet yourself wherever you are in your journey – even if that means you are going backwards to find yourself, because you need to know your journey will not be a straightforward path. It will be made up of twists and turns, roundabouts, and places where you will trip and fall. In these moments it is important that you do not get so lost in the weeds that you cannot find your way out. So even if you must backtrack, find yourself and remind yourself that you are enough, that you are smart enough, that you are capable, and that you are strong enough to start again. And know that you and only you can rescue yourself but know that you have proven time and again that you are more than capable of doing so.

Love,

Me, age 39

Amanda Susan Grice

You Are Precious

Hello there, strong soul!

I know you've struggled a lot with the traumas of the past and that you hate having to address yourself as "dear" so I've spared you from having to read "dear" in the greeting. You are a strong soul. I believe that fully. Every pain you faced, and the pain that you will continue to face - all those days when you worried if you'd come out of it sane - keep reaching into your soul. Hope lives there. Grab a hold of it.

I am proud of you making it through the pain. Oftentimes you will ask if anyone really cares, and who is going to save you? You are not alone. You have friends who you could reach out to who will understand you. Reach out to "TJ" and "JA" more. These are your lifelong friends. You will lose friends along the way. Not in the physical sense, but after you built up the courage to sever some ties to friendships that weren't helping your soul, you formed strength. You are forming your character. You know what is good for you. You will start to break the cycle of trauma by standing up for yourself. Stand up for yourself even more than you think you should. Never apologise for addressing things you know are wrong, just because you want to please a lover or a friend.

You will run into many toxic people in your life. You may think you can change them. You cannot. You will fail at this. You are not meant to be their saviour. Addiction comes in many forms. You'll start to notice this pattern in others, as you recover from your own addiction. You know which one I speak of. Beware of those closest to you. You are a magnet for these unhealthy souls who will look to you to save them as they try to run away from their destructive patterns. Please get away from them. You do not need their "friendship". You are worthy. You just haven't started acting like you deserve this worthiness.

Strong soul, you are precious more than you realise. Please wake up to the fact that what your parents did does not have to define your life. Seek therapy even before you start dating. If possible, see an EMDR specialist right away. This will change your life before there's too much damage done beyond your childhood traumas.

Do not look for love online. That is the most unwise decision I want to prevent you from doing right at this moment. You will not start to date until you are finished with college. You are not missing anything from online dating! I am 110% sure of this. You will save yourself so much heartache.

Remember that you did not provoke what dad and mom did to you. They did not protect you. EMDR therapy will help with unpacking these feelings of suicide and feeling dirty. Seek a therapist before you agree to have sex with any random person, just because you are feeling sorry for yourself. Love does not come from sex. That is a stupid band-aid that the world lies to everyone about. You are so precious. I am repeating myself; you must believe this. YOU ARE SO PRECIOUS! Start believing what your soul is telling you. Not the lies that dad and mom told you.

You will make it out just fine. God is on your side. Your sweet friends are on your side. You will meet plenty of good souls who become your foundation and your family. Embrace them. Hold them close. Be grateful. Your heart will heal with their love poured out to you.

Remember what your late cousin Virgenia told you about what she learned for the "5 simple rules to be happy":

1. Free your heart from hatred

2. Free your mind from worries
3. Live simply
4. Give more
5. Expect less

Hold onto those good memories of those who have passed away. Keep their souls alive by emulating what they taught you. Let go of the bad. Heal your heart from the bad.

Justina

Dear Future Entrepreneur

Dear Future Entrepreneur,

Congratulations to you! I praise you for reaching this far. I know it is not an easy task, but you made it. Your showing great strength of character and dedication through your journey. You are doing a superb job, keep pushing and "Shoot for the stars and aim for the moon" my son says. I know it was heart breaking and a worrying time when mum and dad separated but you are not alone. I know the transition moving home, living in a single parent family home, and becoming a carer was tough but you were fantastic being a young carer. I must remind you that you did a wonderful and loving thing at a young age for someone who needed your support right there and then. Mum would say "if you do good, good will follow you".

At the time it was confusing and tough. I know you wanted to be with friends to enjoy what teenagers do, but you were not given the choice. Instead, you matured quickly and developed into a young carer. It was hard dealing with being a carer, learning to cook, clean, go shopping alone, as well as the separation. Do you remember every Sunday the blue van came to collect you to take you to Sunday school to praise the Lord singing "yes, Jesus loves me," eating patties? Your parents instilled the Lord within you. People have lots to say about God, Jesus but you know there is a strong energy that is guiding you, protecting you, and keeping you strong maybe it is God. You always call to God in times of need. Why do you say "God help us" or "Jesus, help me" anything with the Lord's name in it?

BE WHO YOU DESIRE TO BE…

Remember when you used to babysit, collect children from school, and help children with their homework? You were starting your journey not knowing. You wanted to help others. You were great at it and it felt nice nurturing children and watching them blossom over time. At the same time, school was good, you gained knowledge and achieved good GCSE grades even though you had to mature quickly to care for others. Despite your encounters in your childhood and pressures as a young child, it got too much and slightly pushed you off the rails. You did not want to listen to anyone anymore. But 'thank God' that did not last for long, somehow you changed the way you thought, and this changed you to want better.

YOU HAVE WHAT IT TAKES TO RISE & BEGIN YOUR DREAMS…

You should be proud of you! You realised knowledge is key, it is power over self. You always aspired to be a Computer Programmer when you left school. You wanted to work, earn your own money, and buy your own things. You worked in a supermarket, met people, and 'networked'. You then later completed college and decided to end your supermarket job to begin new adventures. In 2000 you became a mother at 19, enjoyed motherhood, was a carer and accomplished a range of training to develop your skills. Who said being a parent and a carer stops you from learning? You got a new job working for the DSS, you did not enjoy this job, but you stayed and pushed through, networked and you made a good friend. You knew this job was not your pathway sitting in the office and typing away at the computer. You push for a job that was most natural to you.

You headed back to the drawing board and applied for not one but two jobs. Good on you! A School Nurse Assistance, and a Community Auxiliary Nurse. You were naturally drawn to caring work. Can you remember, you really wanted the School Nurse job but was told you were not successful but was successful with the Auxiliary Nurse job. You gained a new challenge to work with the elderly. At the time, 4 years was a long time working in a job. The thing is you enjoyed it.

Again, you were drawn to working with children. You knew you needed concrete knowledge and that paper to show confirmation to firms. Working with children is your passion. So, you went back to college to study a childcare course. You did not give up. You continued to work for the NHS, and you volunteered working in a nursery. With all of this, you were carrying your second child. You know you were amazing, right? Remember when you met other students on the course, and one tried to change your vision as she too was pregnant? But you were determined not to follow her route. You knew you wanted to be someone recognisable to society. You persevered and completed the course and gained your qualification and had your baby. You enjoyed achieving, you enjoyed being a mother, carer and reaching where you needed to be but did not believe it was enough. You went back to college, gained more knowledge about teaching, completed an Access course, which opened doors to University. You did it. Who guided you? Your inner self, that voice in your head reminding you that you can achieve, you can be what you want to be.

Again, you met new people and had another friend, who at the time, put me off completing the degree as you were unwell from a terrible fall while roller skating. This was a crucial time. Do you listen to them or do you persevere and finish what you destined to be? You were heading in the right direction; you were achieving because you furthered your education and studied in depth about children. You made the right choice. When it came to the end of the course you graduated successfully. Be proud of yourself.

NEVER LET ANYONE DISCOURAGE YOUR PASSION & POWER...

Family, friends, colleagues in life will have a different mindset to you but that's okay. Steer clear from someone who is pessimistic. You know your desire; how persistent you can be and your strength. Be diplomatic, be kind, be empathic, remain mentally healthy and resist the juicy gossip. You've worked hard over the years, worked in many different educational settings such as mainstream schools, private schools, a special need school, a hospital school, children centres and nurseries. All the creative things you created; colleagues were envious.

They hated that you'd done a fantastic job caring and pushing children to be the best they can be. Some used all that was within their power, knowing that they wanted to destroy your creative work but never succeeded. You persevered and still won. Ella Fitzgerald said "Just don't give up trying to do what you really want to do. Where there is love and inspiration, I don't think you can go wrong." Did you know your childhood was the foundation to your dreams? You always reached for stars but now you're destined for the moon.

BE PASSIONATE ABOUT YOUR DREAM, BE YOU, BELIEVE & ACHIEVE...

Fast forward to 2016, you finally begin your venture by securing premises, however you faced more challenges, which fell through, but you persevered over the years and finally in 2020 you secured premises. You built your team and started your nursery. You faced many challenges along the way and stumbled upon a Rogue Landlord, your landlord. You were saddened deeply by this. "Who feels it, knows it" as my mother would say. You will feel defeated but "dust yourself off and try again" my father said. Remember knowledge is key! Martin Luther King Jr said, "Let no man pull you low enough to hate him".

Regardless of all your obstacles, you are back on task searching for a new building and feel encouraged to fulfil your venture. Remember, do not give up! You are destined for greatness. You have overcome challenges and opened doors for new things to happen. Surround yourself with knowledgeable people and learn new things all the time.

I hope my words have inspired, encouraged, energised, and showed that resilience gets you to your goals despite difficulties.

OVERCOME FEARFUL THOUGHTS, REACH YOUR DREAM, DON'T GIVE UP & SHINE.

I wish you great success.

Charmaine

You Are Beautiful

Dear Beautiful Younger Self,

I want to tell you how beautiful you are.

Although I knew I was loved by my family (I never ever had any doubt about the depth of Moma and Popa's love for me. They moved mountains to protect, provide and nurture me) I never thought I was beautiful. I grew up not seeing the reflection in the mirror that I now realise other people saw. What I saw in the mirror had no resemblance and aligned with all the other reasons why shyness infiltrated my life. Younger Self, I am writing this to ensure you break that and see your actual beauty.

Although you don't look like your school friends as you are tall, broad, pear shaped, wearing braces and what Jamaicans call a "brownin," you are beautiful.

Although you do not act like your peers because you are not bold, boisterous or part of the trendy "in crowd," you are beautiful.

How do I know? Because your beauty is vividly internal and so strong that it shines through your solid bones, layers of flesh and delicate skin. You are not physically unattractive, but even if you were, your internal beauty is so powerful that it changes your external. This is in the same way that someone who may look externally attractive soon becomes ugly if they show signs of a nasty personality.

When you walk, do not lower your eyes. Oh I know you may do that to reduce the number of times you trip over your big feet. But trust yourself, have confidence in yourself, take one gracious step at a time as your feet are in proportion to your body and God has made them strong enough to carry the rest of you. Raise your head and look forward at the wonderful path ahead of you. Perhaps then you will see and appreciate those eyes of admiration.

Younger Self, on the occasions when you did raise your head, I know you saw the proud glances, but you chose not to appreciate them. You chose to think people were weird or crazy to show an interest in you. I am asking you to alter that perception. Remove the fear and give people a chance and opportunity to see the real you that is inside.

Don't act shy, because that's what it is an "act". By acting that way, you will miss out on many opportunities to walk through amazing doors that are just waiting for you to approach. Upon approach, make sure you actually consider, assess the risk and then walk boldly on through.

Oh Younger Self, you can achieve so much, but I want you to experience the profound joy of happiness. Your happiness comes from within you. It's radiant and glows.

Pay attention to science because research has proven that half of your happiness comes from the genes of Moma and Popa and they are excellent strong genes. They are proven to be resilient to endure the struggles they faced. And not only them, but your grandparents, great grandparents, great great grandparents and many more before them.

A tiny proportion, only 10% comes from your circumstances, so there is no need to spend a huge proportion of your energy to dwell on them in pity parties. Then the rest which is a significant 40% is dependent on your behaviour. Younger Self, you have so much that you are in control of. You can choose and control your own habits. That should make your smile broad from ear to ear.

So Younger Self, what happiness habits are you going to form that will accentuate your beauty even further? Gratitude is a great habit. Be grateful for all you have. Did you know that grateful people feel more positive emotions, a way to maintain your gratefulness is by writing in your gratitude journal each day. Younger Self, I look forward to reading this as I know it will bring joy.

Generosity is powerful so be a cheerful giver. Give from your heart and you will be happier and kinder than many others. Your confidence will flow and you will have an amazing sense of freedom. Your life will gain purpose by what you give and how you help others.

Build strong solid relationships. Relationship is key. You don't need many friends, just ensure that the ones you have are quality and remain in contact with them, especially your solid school friends as they will become your extended family.

Be responsible for your actions, remember, happiness is a choice and you can choose to be happy. Don't allow anyone to steal this choice from you. Stay in control of your choices. Choose joy.

Appreciate all that's around you. Pause and take time to see the beauty that's around you and your beauty will reflect it. There is definitely something to be said about seeing the glass half full.

Oh Younger Self, I need to tell you this before its too late. Well, if you have had any negative thoughts, they are all imprinted in your mind and cannot be erased. Sorry about that. But there is good news!!! You can create new positive thoughts that can leave fresh imprints in your brain. Isn't that exciting? Start from right now.

Healthy habits are good. Ensure you drink plenty water, take regular exercise and eat the greens on your plate.

Younger Self, the best habit you can form is speaking with God on a regular basis. Build that relationship with Him. He loves you. He provides your peace. He sees your beauty. He is love.

Much love,

Beautiful Self

Rona Anderson

Be Confident

Dear Younger M,

There are so many things I want to share with you. Always put God first and never doubt Him. He is always with you, even when you feel or think that He isn't.

Never be afraid to speak up when you feel something isn't right. You will want to fit in with the cool crowd but stand out as you are meant to lead. You will have a testimony as you are one.

When challenges come about, face them with confidence knowing that you will overcome them with the victory. Always hold your head high no matter what. You will make mistakes but use them as lessons for you and to help others.

You will be talked about and judged and it will hurt but don't allow what others say or think about you to discourage you from knowing who you are and whose you are. Know that something good will always come out of something bad. Do not allow negativity to cloud your thinking and judgement.

Be confident in your walk and your talk. Speak positive no matter what you see, hear, think, or feel. Never procrastinate!!!

Don't ever compare yourself to someone else as you don't know what they have faced on their journey to where they are now. Always give 100% to everything you put your mind and hands to. Always try something new.

Go after your goals and when it may seem hard, push harder. You are a light to someone, so shine bright!!!

Do you know why you're waiting to get married? You're doing this to honour God and your future husband. It won't be easy as you will be tempted but do not give up or give in.

No, everybody's not having sex so don't feel as if you have to. You will be looked at differently because you're a virgin but use that as motivation to stay strong!!

So, remember that when you are older and look back, you'll be glad that you decided to wait!! You are unique, charming, strong, loving and so much more. I love you so much!

E.M

You Can Get Here From There

It looks daunting, doesn't it? All that space and unknown ahead of you? But you've never been afraid of exploring. In fact, you relish the idea of stepping off the beaten path and paving your own. Since you were a child, you've dreamed of a life of adventure, of escaping your small town and seeing the world.

You HAVE been afraid of disappointing others though. You've been at war internally, toeing the line between following your heart and passions while being the 'socially acceptable' daughter and sister your family (and let's be honest – society overall) thinks you should be. Here's the truth though. You'll never be both. The two are simply too much at odds. You want to question, you want to know, and you want to create change. That's what you do. Disturbing the peace, throwing up mirrors, and capsizing the status quo wherever you go. And that's ok. YOU are ok. Just the way you are. The world needs that, and YOU. You can't outrun yourself (though you will try on more than one occasion). No matter where you go, you're always going to be there with you so you might as well get used to who you are and embrace it.

Nevertheless, you will still spend decades of your life trying to squeeze some part of yourself into the one-sized mould society offers you – an attractive, smart girl should find a husband, settle down (preferably in the suburbs, though it's ok if you start out in a city), and have a family. Except you don't want any of that. You want to feel that wind in your hair, sailing those unchartered waters (though not figuratively because – spoiler alert – despite years of sailing, twirling on a gymnastics mat, and flipping around on roller coasters with no problems, you will suddenly start experiencing major episodes of motion sickness in your early 20s, which will never abate). You love dirt; to feel the grass and dirt under your toes. You love the smell of the rain. You love sweat.

People will bully you. Call you weird. Quirky. Someone to keep at arm's length. Except they will want your kinetic energy and your creative mind. You're a vast, fertile imaginative well of ideas that so often acts as the catalyst for progress and action, for building bottom lines and bringing in success. And people will want to bottle that up and throw the rest of you away. It will fester inside you for years, this anger at those who made it a point to hurt you. Your deep well of strength and willpower will carry you through, even when you are firmly convinced you cannot go on another day. Even when you don't think you have any strength left. Remember, you have (and will) hurt people. You might not mean it. You might think you are justified. And sometimes you will be. But you will hurt them, nonetheless. Glass houses are everywhere you look.

Society will remind you of your weaknesses and faults, the many ways you aren't 'the norm.' And for a long time, you will let it get to you. Because you are human. And because it is so very hard to NOT feel that sense of shame and self-loathing when millions of signs and signals around you tell you that you are less than, a failure. But you are neither. You have fallen, yes. Many times. And you've gotten yourself up and dusted yourself off and kept going. You've tacked and jibed (maybe occasionally before or after the optimum time, but nobody's perfect) and navigated all kinds of seas, making you a formidable sailor.

But you cannot always sail alone. We all need our tribe. And that is the one lesson that will take you the longest to learn. Despite longing for your 'people,' you will spend way too much time looking in the wrong places because you will still be learning to love yourself.

You will cry yourself to sleep at night enough times to make the Nile overflow. You'll sleep in cars when you simply don't know where to go and you can't face seeing another person. You'll get lost in the woods, figuratively and literally, as you do your best to shut out the noise of a world that doesn't seem to want you as you are. But you will keep going.

Because you will find acceptance and love at all levels and of all kinds. Love from strangers who take you in and become family. Love from friends who, despite distance and time, will stand by you and hold out a hand no matter how many times you slap it away (and you do, often). Love from partners who might not be the right fit for a lifetime but are the right fit for at least a short time and will fill your heart with the highs and lows that only honest, authentic love can offer. You will often feel alone, but when you stop and ask, you will always find those to travel that bumpy road right alongside you. Those who believe in you and who you believe in. Because it isn't a one-way street, my dear. You must give as much as you get. And though you are a giver at heart, you aren't soft. And that can make you harder, for many people, to understand and appreciate. Your strong personality and emotional armour will overshadow your soft underbelly and keep many from getting too close. In some ways you will lament that - that people are intimidated by you – and in other ways, you will celebrate it. Because it's the ones who took the time to get to know you, who weren't scared by your bark, who admired your tenacity and your earnestness and your desire to act, who will still be there for years to come. It is also that same tenacity, earnestness, and willingness to act that will enable you to succeed when the world tells you you should fail.

You will forever either inspire or infuriate others. Loved for your courage and tenacity; hated for your courage and tenacity. Loved for your looks; hated for your looks. Loved for your talent; hated for your talent. Loved for your backbone; hated for your backbone. There will never be middle ground, no matter how hard you try to find it, and all the searching is a waste of energy you cannot afford. Accept it and just let it be.

Your belief in your ability to figure things out will guide you, sometimes into situations that are legitimately life or death. And you will survive, but you will pay consequences, forced into places where you cannot thrive, in jobs and roles that don't challenge you, or that challenge you in all the wrong ways. You will seek out new situations to remedy that. Sometimes you will succeed; sometimes you won't. But you will always keep searching, on a never-ending quest to find the 'right thing.' It will take you many years to realise that the 'right thing' is whatever you want it to be. You don't find it. You create it.

All of this is not to tell you to do things differently. Making different choices might shield you from an immense amount of pain and struggle, but I can't say I would do it. For one, if I did that, you wouldn't end up here. And even now, despite the struggles, I'm not sure if here is a bad thing. It isn't easy. It will never be easy. Doing what you care about and staying true to yourself in a world that tells you to conform will NEVER be easy. But that's not a good reason not to do it. Because despite the challenges, your life will also be full of profound beauty and unique experiences other people dream of having but never do because they chose to play it safe while you did not.

You will have to make choices you don't like. You will have to give up things you care about to get to other things you care about. You will have to walk away from places and people to grow into the person you need to be. It will hurt. You will hurt, sometimes so much you want to hurt yourself. You will cry and scream and rage and howl at that moon. You will survive. And you will laugh and smile and love and find joy in millions of moments so precious they make all the pain worthwhile. You will bring happiness and inspiration to others, and they will do the same for you.

You will see the world, living on three different continents, working in jobs and locations people dream about, and tasting the kaleidoscope of flavours life has to offer.

Oh, and you will be bitten by a cheetah. Don't worry – you'll be fine. And every warrior needs their battle scars, right? It's the price we pay for living life out loud. Keep doing it. Because even though you will so often feel it isn't the case and you will doubt yourself in every way imaginable - your abilities, your talents, your ideas, your purpose, your reason for existing at all - the world needs your light. Shine on.

Jennifer Vitanzo

This Too Shall Pass

Dear Phoenix,

I know this letter finds you well.

Reflecting back is like standing from the top of a mountain and feeling we've come a long way.

We have done it! We will continue to do more and more.

We will always do and be better.

The phrase of a lifetime is "if only we could have known then, what we know now" this phrase speaks volumes to so many aspects of life.

I write this letter to you, that although neglected self-care was a major spiral for some of the pit falls along the way, I felt you should know the importance of your duality in this. Even at a tender age, you always strived for self–improvement, but sometimes this meant being self-sacrificial. Yet, you persevered no matter what setbacks you faced.

I want you to know you sincerely helped me to embody determination and courage that stands above and beyond my own minds limitations of what was and what is possible.

You are the fire of my passion and drive for knowledge, grounding and ultimately healing.

I know from personal experience the situations you have been through, most of which you downplayed, overlooked and turned a blind eye too.

Those moments when you realised only you have your own back.

When you started to see the illusions for what they truly were, many people in your company, but still isolated and alone. You see no one could relate to you in your situation except older people, by the way, it wasn't that you were weird, why you didn't fit in, it was because you were so different.

In chaotic situations, you had to think and act quickly, let's not forget those moments when you neglected your self-care and mental health for the sake of a job, relationship or some other situation where you didn't put your best interests first because you were too fearful of the consequences of diving into the unknown.

Standing here 20 years in the future, I know how far you've come.

Remember that time, the very first time, you actively put yourself first?!

At just, 17 years old and going through a traumatic time, so many changes! You had recently become a teenage mother, trying to continue training and helping your mum. Not to mention the abusive relationship you had going on and being diagnosed with a medical condition.

I remember you feeling that you had something to prove, people had you pinned as someone who would be falling into an abyss of darkness, as if your life was over.

In their minds the coffin was sealed.

You tried your hardest not to believe them, although sometimes you doubted yourself, you had to grow thick skin, and put your head down and focus.

Thank you with all my heart for having indestructible self-belief during this time, this experience helped so much in later life; this was the platform for us to build resilience and perseverance.

Do you remember the bombshell dropped, when your mother announced she was moving over 4 hours away with her new family? I remember you feeling abandoned and isolated, but pretending to be happy.

You bottled everything up, like it wasn't happening.

I know you feared the thought of change and being alone.

Honouring your self-care, you actually decided to take time out to gather your thoughts, to escape reality. You planned a visit to Bristol with your best friend, your first trip without guidance.

You stayed away until you knew your mum was gone, so you didn't have to see the process of her leaving

The day of your return home, by far was the hardest; when you came into an empty house, with most of the furniture gone.

I wish I could have held you so tight that day as you sobbed at the foot of the stairs; I wish I could have told you at that very moment, something I learned "This too shall pass" it will make sense as you continue, I hope it resonates with you, and does to this day!

It's something valuable I have learned over the years to ease the overthinking and anxiety when faced with trauma and changes.

This fable has served me well "This too shall pass." I have found this really captures perspective that everything is always moving in life and just as there are bad times, there will certainly be good times.

Looking back, I wish I could tell you that you are strong and resilient and that what people do or say isn't a reflection of you, but them. I wish we could have had a conversation, where I could have reassured you, that if you put your mind to it, you could realign and make progress.

I want you to know that the difficulty you have faced was actually the making of whom you are now and you should be proud to be a person, who in the face of adversity and trauma continues to rise up. It is incredible to be a person who takes responsibility for their actions and has not allowed life to make them bitter.

These very experiences have made you adaptable, strategic and to this very day you're able to radiate joy and light. You have lit the way for others who lack motivation through their own perceptions of limitations, given them confidence to make beautiful changes to their life and in turn you have flourished at anything you have put your mind too.

The mystical universe works in mysterious ways, as a child and into your early teens, you lived in chaos, you always had to be the responsible one. Don't play it down, that on many occasions you were presented with domestic violence in an unstable home environment. Despite your circumstances you strived in school.

Where we stand now, we recognise that our parents were both facing trauma of their own and had a hard, difficult life. Although you didn't understand then, you recognised that as such, they could only love you to the best of their ability and understanding from their perception of love.

Although this impacted you greatly; I am proud you never held it against your parents and poisoned your heart against them.

To this day we look after our parents and have learned to truly forgive them for their transgressions against myself and siblings.

What we have learned from this is that although hurt can cause resentment, these types of feelings are not good to carry in our heart. They weigh heavy on the mind.

We have to honour our own feelings and wellbeing, taking time to be still.

Another point to recognise and honour is that when trauma occurs, your emotions are valid, you just needed to learn not to release at your breaking point. In hindsight, we have learned feelings need to be dealt with proactively.

The universe working mysteriously knew that when your mother left, it was a way for you to go into retrospection and isolation to pick up the pieces of your life.

You definitely had something to prove and you have done an amazing job.

I am so proud of you.

You kept going; at 17 years old, you were determined, inventive and used your initiative to get by, you strived at this stage, and you knew where we wanted to go.

I always admired your ability to know when it was time to put your mind to something and step by step you made progress to it and it was done.

Fast forwarding to the present, I want you to know that you have only had something to prove to yourself.

This is the true art of continuous self-improvement.

I absolutely love how you have followed your heart with travelling and experiencing different parts of the world.

Your creativity has always been an outlet, thank you for acknowledging this from an early age.

I love how you were able to step out of your comfort zone and look after yourself and children, I love how independent and determined you are.

I only have to think of some of the situations you faced in the past to be motivated today, I can't express enough how much you have inspired me to keep going, no matter how hard things look.

In a dedication to all the situations where we never put ourselves first; I honour you daily by taking time out to be a part of many self-care platforms of creativity and physical endurance.

I am blessed to still have the energy to keep up with such an inquisitive soul; I am never short of an adventure or mystery.

I have only you to thank for helping me get to where I am now and where I may go from this point on. My platform will be from your courage and motivation.

I consider myself very lucky to have seen the world from your eyes and I look forward in life thanks to you.

Wishing you every success, you truly deserve it.

Phoenix

You Are Treasure Not Trash

Dear Younger Soul,

You are fearfully and wonderfully made, but you haven't yet realised that – at 18 you are still desperate to find love, and feel loved. You secretly crave those wolf whistles as cars pass you by on the street, and slow dances as the club comes to a close at night. You don't yet know that that attention isn't an affirmation of how beautiful you are, it's simply a measure of how desperate a man is to hold a woman in his arms that night, but only for that night. It could be another woman. Any woman. Some woman. But never his woman. Never you.

You see, all women have a cost. The cost denotes their value. Those that come into a man's arms too easily, are considered too cheap. Cheap women are easily purchased, used and discarded, so a man learns to treat them with little value. The greater the cost, the higher her value. The higher her value, the more she is wanted, and treasured once she is won. You see, a man will always see treasure, but he will only ever know the value of that treasure once you teach him how valuable that treasure actually is.

But your heart craves to be treasured so much that the only currency you see yourself as having is what a man sees. You've yet to understand that treasure and value are two separate things. One is easily seen, another is worked out. That is why, 'one man's treasure can be another man's side piece'. But rarely can one man's side piece ever be another man's treasure. Because once a woman is truly valued by a man, it is rare she will ever be willing to be another man's trash.

Don't believe the feminist agendas that claim sexual liberation is the answer to patriarchal oppression. Don't believe them when they say that you will feel better by trying to adopt an attitude of dismissing emotional entanglements in intimacy. Don't believe that one night stands are the answer to filling the void. That chasm can only be filled by your first true love, and you've yet to meet him. He crafted you together whilst in your mother's womb, and He has already set aside a man that will show you unconditional love like you have never known it.

By your nature you are designed to enjoy safe, secure, and committed intimacy within a union of mutual respect and trust. You are designed for marriage. It is not outdated. It is not a pipe dream. If a man doesn't see your value enough to marry you first, sharing yourself with him before will do nothing but send your emotions into a tail spin of uncertainty.

Somehow you think by sharing yourself with Mr. Club Night man, he will see how valuable your treasure, how valuable the currency, and want to invest in a future together. Sadly, he will not. Because as beautiful as you are, your greatest currency comes from within you. You do not wear it. He isn't seeing your value, he is seeing your insecurity. Right now, even you cannot see your true value, so how can anyone else evaluate the value of your treasure?

Contrary to popular culture, sexual liberation isn't achieved by liberally sharing your currency with little thought for your value. A real treasure doesn't need to be shared before it's worth is seen. A real treasure doesn't compete with others to be picked. It stands out. It know's its worth. It stands alone. So don't be disappointed when you are the only friend not picked for a dance at the end of the night. Maybe those men looking on can see the treasure in you that you cannot yet see.

Don't be worried when the wolf whistles are pointed at others, whilst men pass you by. Maybe they can see what you are yet to discover, you are too valuable to be picked, used and discarded. You are worth more than rubies and gold. And in a few years from now you will begin to see just how much of a treasure you truly are.

Tee Tee Sampson

It's Not Your Fault

Dear Joy,

I know today was a horrible day, the home you had come to love so much, which gave safety, has been invaded and you along with it. It would be the last time you slept with the lights on. The bliss of forgotten sexual abuse trauma, you hoped you would never have to face again, has opened up like pandora's box. You are walking on the line of two worlds and your young self is being destroyed by both.

This is the day, you truly ceased yourself from having a relationship with yourself and humans. You made a way into an acting career without awards, or just maybe the award came in the form of you being able to keep living in the world and not give way to the death-calling loud whispers.

I don't blame you for what you had to do to survive daily, in a world that placed you body for auction, to the cruelest animals. I am very proud of you Joy.

It might sound a little strange but you never wasted your pain and trauma. You don't know it yet, but there's all the writings you did, hiding them between folded clothes and boots. It will make sense in the future. You channelled all your emotions into your pen and stage, it was the only time you truly could breathe.

You turned all that pain and trauma into art, you became an impressive actress at school (loving improv, the most) and would irritate mom on few occasions, with you constant rehearsals at home. An example, you set the scene and decided to play a blind child, mom's face was filled with confusion but you didn't give way and continued. Her expression was that of, either you were going to get yelled at or totally ignorant of you. She chose to indulge you and said "not all blind people have their eyes closed." It would be one of the only couple of times she peeked into your creative side. You spent the next few days, honing your skills to act blind with your eyes open.

It might have been torturous to talk about what happened to you and everything you were feeling but your art spoke for you.

There are a few reasons I chose to write to you, a day after this traumatic event. It laid the groundworks for your most dramatic and effective change. A part of you began to question a lot of things, even as you were shutting down. You began to understand that 'house games' were not the norm and family could also hurt you. You had to protect yourself, even if it meant not being able to connect to humans.

What happened to you was not your fault. Joy what happened to you was not your fault. Everything you thought was wrong with you, would be what saves you. Your mind would be one of your greatest weapons, especially your refusal to be put in a box. Your teachers were 100% wrong about you. You are not stupid, they simply lacked the knowledge to understand an active creative mind as yours.

God gave you the gift of your creative mind to help you breathe before you would come to know him and call Him Daddy God. He is the love of your life and truly helped to heal you and continues to heal because it is a daily journey.

I love you Joy, very much and I end this letter with one of the poems you will come to write about the events of the previous night. It was very challenging but with Daddy God by your side, you did and I do believe it is beautifully written.

Cold 1999

My tiny hands handcuffed to his
Separated from my mother
I have never needed her more
He took me
Being led to the slaughter
Of fine décor of my living room
I wondered at my fear
Of sleeping in the dark

I lived in a house converted
To headquarters for dad
Because it was too big for four people
But he was determined to have it
And I conquered every space
To find the best hiding place
But today I was the one being conquered

For a second I find the courage
To look into his eyes
It was normal; welcoming but empty
As we made our way
To the place that echoed
Laughter for a 1000 miles
It was made silent by the resounding
Slaps that made my ears
Ring for a week
When I dared to plead for mercy
From his carnal ways

I could be his daughter or little sister
I wondered as I gazed at the
White ceiling shaped like little boxes
Imagining a better world of peace
But I crash landed back to earth
By every brute force
And my core shaking like an earthquake

Don't move he said
As he made himself decent
To my immobile body
That did not need his command

J Clyne

Love Yourself

Hi gorgeously beautiful, younger me,

I know you've never heard that before but accept it. You are, and you deserve to hear it. You'll learn later that you are fearfully and wonderfully made by God, and that, my darling, is where your greatest amount of beauty comes from. You've always loved the fact that you were 'dedicated to God' rather than Christened, so know how much God loves you and thinks you are great. You need to remember this when you look at yourself in the mirror and when you hear people say negative things about the way you look.

It's unfortunate that praise is not highly regarded in your circles of influence. People in and outside of the home want you to do well, but often use a stick rather than a carrot to achieve this. It's also sad that sometimes, adults are not more careful with their words, and other children think it's cool to find a weak spot and pick at it. Especially as you are going to develop early.

This is going to mean that you gain weight and are a little heavier than your friends. You'll start your periods early and your breasts will be bigger than the average for your age. Remember when you put tennis balls in your top? Well, you'll never have to do that again! Instead, you'll be teased for developing early and even family will tease you, but you are just growing up. It's called puberty.

Stop dieting! I know you've tried a couple times already, but stop. Instead, ditch the young girl magazines and learn about healthy foods, stay active and just love every bit of yourself, no matter what. That will help more than any diet, but like I have already said, you are going through puberty, so you are fighting a short-term issue with a long-term solution that will only serve to make you focus far too much on something that will just increase your anxiety around your identity.

Furthermore, the more attention you give this, the more detrimental it will become. Low self-worth will increase, and soon you'll see the girls and women in the magazines and think *you* should change. However, you'll eventually discover that either the image is not real or they have to go through terrible things to look like they do, but I've said already, you are just growing up. These are your curves, designed by God.

Ignore the boys and men that compliment you on your face or figure. You are only 12 years old. They know it, even if they pretend they don't and for some it's a way to prime you and open you up to the world of sex far earlier than you should even be thinking about it. You already have a lot to think about. And in any case, they are just not sincere. Their interest is for the wrong reason, don't rush to grow up because it feels so bad to be young in a growing body. Don't resent those around you that are trying to protect you. You don't yet realise that the priming is also helping to encourage you to feel like they are stopping you from entertaining fun. Change that for an F in foolishness because that is actually what you are missing out on.

Love yourself, Mo (a shortened version of your name that you will hate until you are over 35 years old, because you feel old and that adds to your already low self-esteem) and see yourself as God sees you; a special young lady who has a bright future ahead of her. You are not just your body and you are more than your bust, as you grow, you'll even out. The size you despise in your teens, will be the size you desire in your 20's and 30's and beyond. Go figure.

It's confusing, I know. Some mock you and others want to touch you, but I say again, you are more than your body. I'm repeating myself because one negative comment can kill 10 positive ones and the world has a lot to say to you. And those in close proximity, who have hardly anything nice to say at all, are often presenting to you nothing more than a representation of the negativity they feel about themselves.

They'll want to tell you you're too fat, you're too big, you're too busty. So of course, when an offer of intimate touching arrives it's received as a sign of acceptance of your shape and not as the opportunistic letching that it is. But I say again, you are just growing. Don't let these negative things get inside your head because it will affect you for a long time. You're too beautiful to be affected like this by things people say without thinking about what they are saying.

I say again, you are fearfully and wonderfully made by an Almighty God that makes no mistakes. He planned the time you'd arrive and the way you would look. He loves you, as do your parents. God's love is unconditional. You are more than your looks but you look great.

Never forget and keep at the front of your mind that you're created in His image and likeness, you are super creative, super talented, you'll be able to juggle and do multiple things.

You want to be free-spirited but must learn discipline.

That discipline includes not allowing yourself to stay focussed on negative thoughts. You must see the negativity like weeds; they grow fast, they grow wild, they look like they belong but they overtake and overshadow everything else. They take over the rich fertile ground that is your mind and drain it of its resources. So be disciplined in your thinking. If you get your thinking right, everything else will fall into place.

Here's something that will help you as you go along; One man's treasure is another mans trash, what does that mean? It means that one person might not like what you do or say but another will love it. The fact is, you are a part of a puzzle, in fact you are a solution to someone's problem. You are all round great. You are not perfect but you are great. So love yourself, ALL of yourself

Maureen

Got Your Back Like A Rucksack

Hey Lady,

If you're reading this, it means it has happened again. It's okay, because we've got your back like a rucksack. So now, we are going to throw down, some reminders as to why,

You = Love!

In no particular order:

- Yes, you may believe you have two left feet, but that beat, that pumps inside your heart, move to THAT rhythm.

- Never stop smiling, I'm serious, no matter what may come your way always smile. "Smile a while and give your face a rest" If you can, Laugh! We know your laugh is infectious, once you get going. We have the internal stomach muscles to prove it.

- Try some brand-new foods, yep, even the disgusting tasting ones you had as a child. Ackee and Saltfish is a must, and Egg is your new best friend.

- Stand in front of a mirror, in fact, any reflective surface where you can see yourself bounced back, and take a good look in it. Check YOU out! You see that beautiful human being standing there, that my dear is…

- YOU! You beauty! Never forget how beautiful YOU are!

- Never stop dreaming, always have ambitions and always work towards your own goals.

- To Clarify for anyone that missed it Chicken IS LIFE!!!

- Life, is out of our hands, sometimes we experience heavy hits and loses, but Lady, do NOT let it stop you, use it to fuel you.

- Make the most of the present, it is here that you will have the most fun. We cannot change the past, but we can adjust the blueprints of our future.

- Go on adventures, take leaps into the unknown, and jump straight into muddy puddles.

- Never, ever, ever, stop singing, even when you think/feel you are maybe out of tune, off pitch, struggling to hold your breath. Fun Fact: The shower has the best acoustics. It's also one of your greatest forms of release.

- Make sure any labels that you are putting on yourself, are those of your own, (even better Check who God has called you to be) never let anyone's words put you or keep you down.

- Be Silly! 6-year-old you needs to remember the random bursts of the silly faces.

- Never underestimate the importance of a breath. It is one of the first and last gifts of love that God gives to us.

- If you are struggling, talk to someone, put your hand up, wave the white flag, get down on your knees in prayer. Don't suffer in silence.

- Be Teachable, you are not always right.

- Time is something we have no control over, enjoy each moment as it comes, and let it flow freely.

- Be gentle with yourself

- Be kind with yourself

- Be patient with yourself

You are a Queen,

Love you loads and remember,

"We got our Back like a Rucksack!"

Leanne Burrowes

Hope After Heartbreak

Dear Younger Self,

You will experience your very first heartbreak at the tender age of 11. Right now, you don't even know the meaning of heartbreak but later in life, you will understand it fully. You will also learn that everyone has their own definition of heartbreak or heartache based on their own journey and experiences in life. Your first heartbreak will come from someone you love very dearly, your mom. She will say a few harsh words that sounds like this "As big as you are, you should have to pay a boy to sit next to you". This sounds mean, right? Yes, it does, and it is! But this is so far from the truth about you and if you listen closely to what I'm going to tell you, you will not be bound by these words or anyone else's harsh words of untruth.

The first thing that I want you to know before I go any further is that almost everything that you will ever need to confirm about yourself, others and how to navigate the world can be found in the Holy Bible. Learning God's word will help you learn the difference between facts vs. the truth. Facts can change based on the situation or circumstances surrounding it. The truth, God's truth, will NEVER change. The fact in this situation is that, yes, you are a little chunky for an 11-year-old according to the world's standards and the BMI calculator. And yes, a lot of boys probably don't show interest in you currently and that's ok, you're too young for boys anyway. You will have plenty of time to experience boys, and trust me, you don't need to rush it.

The truth in this situation (and lots of other situations down the road) is that God knew you before he created you in your mothers womb and he set you apart, Jeremiah 1:5. You are fearfully and wonderfully made, Psalms 139:14. And my personal favourite is that you are made in God's Image, Gen 1:27. All of these are God's truths about you which means they are your truths and unchangeable. You are royalty and the daughter of the highest King. This means that you are made of everything great so never allow anyone in this world to tell you otherwise. And don't allow yourself to ever speak anything other than greatness out of your mouth about yourself and other people.

The situation with your mom was just the start of your heartbreak but it will not be the last. Throughout this life, you will meet some nice people and some really mean people. You will constantly have people hurt you with their words, actions or both, even people that you trust. But this is all a part of your growth process and it will not break you if you cling to the truth. Embrace the nice people that you cross paths with and learn from the mean ones, pray for them too.

You will also have to keep a heart of forgiveness your whole life and you will have a very long life so sit back and enjoy the journey. Never hold anything against anyone. If you remember to always forgive, you will have a peace within you that most people around you will constantly search for and may never find. It won't always be easy to forgive people that hurt you but remember that the forgiveness will not be for them, it will be for you. When you hold onto unforgiveness, you'll hinder your progress in life and end up taking a longer route to get to the places that were right around the corner.

God has placed a calling on your life to help other people in various ways but mainly through life coaching. In order to be a life coach, you must not only get through things in life (bad and good), but you must go through them and learn the lessons in it. Sometimes you will feel like you can't go on and will want to quit but DON'T. I need you to push through all situations and birth every gift that God has placed on the inside of you, just like a woman in labor.

When a woman is pregnant with a child, she goes through 9 months of carrying the baby. Throughout this time, she is going through physical and emotional changes that aren't always pleasant. She is also preparing for the arrival of her baby so she is putting everything in place (planning) so that when the baby comes, it will have all the necessities. When it is time to give birth, she is in lots of pain and agony. But once she pushes that baby out, the pain is gone and she gets to take home her prize, a beautiful baby. This will be the same for you and your gifts, but you must endure the process and push through the pain when it's time to push. There are people waiting on you to help them, don't let them down.

The last thing that I want to remind you to do is to love everyone and love hard. And don't just love the lovable ones, that's easy but love the unlovable ones too, you will meet plenty of them. God is love and we can't say we love him if we have hatred for other people, 1st John 4:20. This doesn't mean that you must agree with what everyone's does and how they live or allow yourself to be treated unfairly…. no not at all. However, your responsibility is to love them unconditionally just as God loves you, John 15:12. When you find this as a difficult task to do, pray for strength to love them and it will be granted to you. Some, you will even have to love from a distance and that's ok as long as there is no hatred in your heart for them. You will find that there is already enough of that in the world and you don't need to add to it.

You're going to have a long bumpy road ahead of you, storms included. You will also have times of smooth sailing. It will feel as though you're floating through life on cruise control, on a sunny day with no rain cloud in sight. Embrace these moments as they come and take something special from it all. You will succeed no matter what because you were created for this! I love you very very much. Make sure you look in the mirror and repeat "I Love You" to yourself over and over, as often as possible and mean it with ever fiber in you, even when you don't feel loveable.

Sincerely,

Christina.

We Can Get Through This

Darling Me,

Hello. Tell me how you are. Keep telling me how you are. I want to know. Even, and especially, when you truly do not know. When the room spins. When your stomach lurches. I am here with you. I am navigating all things together with you. I am holding your hand. And everything is accepted and understood here. Not because it's comprehensible, formed or misshapen, or anything more than a sense or an echo or a wisp. I am here. I am you. I am your core and I am unshakeable.

It's okay to lose touch with me. It's okay to drift. It makes sense that you may not always have the time, space or inclination to feel your hand in mine. But it is there all the same. I am your truest song, the intuition that reaches for you without thinking. Because I am not thought. And this is hard for you, I know, because you believe that you can control and arrange your experience through the power of your thought. Of making words and connections and images. You want for that to make everything better, and it can, but it is not the whole picture.

Likewise, turning off the thoughts, shutting down, hiding, blocking are very powerful resources at your disposal. And there is a wonder in the capacity of our many modes. I will use these, although I am not in charge. We work as an organism. And sometimes you will shut down.

You will stop in your tracks. You will withhold. You will offer up something in sudden desperation and then pull back away. Fearful of your words. Of how they impact reality. How, perhaps, there is some kind of magic that can make it not have happened, by virtue of not acknowledging it. Or it being acknowledged.

And this might mean that you spend a whole dimension of being caught up in a place that is pooling your resources. That grabs you close and holds you tight and mutters beautiful sounds into your hair as tears drop.

And all of this is okay. All your responses, and strategies. All the ways you get through are to be loved, welcomed and held here from your core. And they may be strategies that are ultimately short term, they may be strategies that exchange one difficulty for another. But they are all okay and they are all welcome here. This is a journey. You may not call it trauma. You may not call it. But don't worry, perspective will continue to unveil itself to you. There is no timetable. This is not linear.

Whether it's months or years, the work will be getting done - sometimes with your active engagement, other times without. And there will come a time when it is with you. For me, that is now. Twenty three years later. I have a good deal of grieving experience. I have been in its tractor beam. The headlights. I have felt irreparable, and frightened and thoroughly unloveable. I have felt awkward, rejected, unheard and presumptuous. And all of that has delivered me here. To this peak of integration where I have moved from passive to active. Where I have felt able to claim my experience and share it with you here. Where I have felt into the part of myself that is holding my hand.

That part that was always there, holding, protecting, waiting. Patient and loving. Radically accepting and wild with unconditional love.

Where I am able to open the windows and doors to the sweet, hurt, gorgeous place and let the breezes swirl and pull at the curtains. Where the piles of papers, anguished in their extraction, can float, lift and scatter. May even flutter like butterflies as they circle you, lifted momentarily, relieved, acknowledged and then released.

Released from the work. From this particular, quiet, hidden work and move it out into the sunlight. Into those sunny days at the park with friends. Cartwheeling and full of beginnings. Because this return to the place where it all stopped is going to come when you are ready, when you are resourced. When it is safe. When the door to the beautiful, secret space can unjam itself and swing open, scattering more of those accumulated papers. Where the deposited work of grieving can be gathered lovingly and burned in your fire of rebirth and renewal. Not because it is finished, but because you know now. It has been integrated. It has made it all the way through you and found its place of honour within your whole and it doesn't need to hide in its quiet, tidy enclave.

And I can share the reams of my experience in few words and climb up the stack, this paper iceberg, to make a whole. A foundation that builds to something slight and wordless and lungs that are filled with the beautiful freshness of this peak of living.

All the sensations, difficult and easy, are the paths that you have taken to arrive here. Incremental, tiny steps. Honouring your experience can bring it here. Trusting and surrendering to something so unfathomable, so much bigger than you and your being, will bring you here in the end. To your voice. To ownership of trauma. To the enormous pay off and sensual completion of a phase.

My adored friend, Ben, died suddenly in a car accident when I was 18. I came to understand, as I pushed through the early years of grief, that I was in a deep and unusual connection to him. What I came to understand as being in love. I felt shame and presumptuous around this posthumous clarity. Two months ago, twenty three years later, I experienced two separate car incidents in the space of three weeks that threw me back into a powerful bodily response. I returned to a state of hyper-vigilance as both driver and passenger. I felt out of control and frightened on every corner I took and began to speak to myself to acknowledge this fear.

Fear not only of the lost confidence in driving, but fear that I was being plunged back into the place I had struggled for so many years. I was revisited. I was able to lean into acknowledging and speaking about it within a wonderful circle of women and experienced the enormity of feeling heard and received. I couldn't have planned for this. I had spent the intervening years managing my grief, learning to love it and house it and hold it. And then, as suddenly as his being gone, I went through a short, intense processing. Of noticing that I could hold this without fear of implosion now. That I had arrived at the place where I could look my love in the eye, without shame, without fear and embrace its phenomenal beauty and gifts. I started to speak it. I started to free it into the world as something of huge value and power. I was returning to the vibrant voice of my youth and pulling it up, through and out of me. I was celebrating the glory of the work and the simplicity of its release.

Laura Smith

Listen To Silence

Listen to Silence, it will reveal more than chatter.
Don't be afraid of shadows, that's all they are, harmless.
Keep the light spirit of your inner child, alive.
Go there, connect with it, which will enable you to let go & laugh.
Giving you freedom to dream bigger & take risks.
Smile more, remember to be grateful, this will remind you of all that you do have.

Let go of situations that you have no control over.
Stop trying to please others by letting yourself down.
Know your worth, cherish your spirit.

Dance more, movement with music is release, it sets you free.
Express yourself without fear of judgement.

Have courage to embark onto new adventures, however bold.

Get out into Nature, it's free. Let it work its magic.
Take deep breaths, this will open your heart. Look at the colours, at your surroundings.
It will fill you with hope, clarity.
Refocusing on what is important. Nature is constantly changing as your life will.

Nothing stays the same. Go with it. Don't resist as it's a waste of valuable time & energy.

Know when you have truly tried hard in relationships but it's not working.
Be true to yourself & walk away, let it go.

No matter what difficulties life throws, you can overcome by changing your thought process.
That power is yours. Its only limits are what you set.
The tools to healing are within you, don't waste time searching.
Sit quietly, & listen to your instincts. It will reveal all that you need.

Meyrem Zekayi

We Are Free

Dear Younger Self,

I heard you slid lamenting into darkness regarding your skin. Stop your weeping, there has been some miss understanding about how you came to be…me…

Cynthia Butler is your name. History has told "You're the product of America's largest Slave Auction known as The Weeping Time!" You were born a tiny brown skin torch, on a cold and grey Winter's Wednesday, as beautiful as can be. A love child, the apple of your Daddy's eyes, right until the day he dies.

Born to a fain family who lived in a green wooded house sitting on bricks by the Flint River. Daddy's the literate sanitation truck driver. Momma's the Yahwistic writer/ housewife. Come Christmas and Easter our house was jovial, full of good food, music, and lots of toys! Even though those were the days Jim Crow ruled, racial tension had peaked an inferno's heat, Civil Rights Movement was at the forefront, and insurgency of many wars were sprouting everywhere. Daddy was a major part of the 60-70's Civil Rights Movement.

That's when you met Attorney. C.B. King in a big room. On one side, you felt the ambiguousness of Sanitation Workers who were on strike, and swelter from fires brewed by White demonstrators burning down the other side.

Then, you couldn't imagine the impact a meeting of this caliber would have on your life. But at that moment in time, you're Daddy's cherubic girl free to play outside. Outside in your neighbourhood where hardened red clay dirt replaced beautiful green grass. Playing hopscotch, hopeful you can jump all the way to 10. Jumping rope, two swung as fast as they can. Playing baseball, going fishing and remember you dressed like a boy then?

Building playhouses made from large cardboard boxes, carving holes as windows and doors, we anchored our homes to mimic the haven where we resided.

Remember that innocent little girl who hated going to bed but loved to wake to the sound of Momma's sweet mantras, "Come On, Little Children Let's Sing About The Goodness Of The Lord!" and a sip of her Maxwell house coffee with cane sugar and Carnation milk? You hurried off to school only to be chased home by mannish boys whose conjuring hands loved to pull your hair!

One Christmas, Daddy buys a bicycle and teaches you how to ride. You rode it to school and back. Fast enough to escape forbidden clasps. Docile as a child, you ran away from boys. Because you have collected fable's your Elders told "Boys aren't nothing but trouble!" And remember when Daddy dropped off that pink bike? You said with that gaudy attitude of yours "Look everybody my Daddy loves no one else but me! I have two bikes come let us go ride!"

But to your surprise this bike wasn't yours! Daddy gave the bike to Mary Helen. Your best friend who lives in the yellow house behind yours. Shrinking as you watch Daddy teach Mary Helen how to ride, you threw a temper tantrum. Wailing very loud, "Mary Helen we share a lot of things but you not going to take My Daddy!

For some childish reason you thought this meant she is your sister! So, you wailed and wailed screaming for days. For some thoughtless reason Daddy figures to ease your crying it's time he introduces you to his other children. Just so happens their mother resembles your mother. Daddy was right, meeting them made you feel a whole lot better.

Once you got home, you hurried to tell Momma the good news and you blurted out "Momma guess who I just met?" Little did you know this was devastating news! Your brokenhearted Momma slid lamenting. Only this time her bruises and sobbing were not from a hellacious fight. Funny when your younger siblings were being born, you thought Momma was on vacation, she always returned with a new baby brother or sister.

And remember when a knock came at the door. It is about your brother Al, marching smack in the middle of a busy intersection. A toddler wearing only a stinky diaper, chanting baby gibberish, "Goo-goo Gaga! Goo-goo Gaga!" as he waves his makeshift flag. Amazingly this little intrepid wanderer stopped traffic!

Most travellers pulled over to the side then joined in sequence chanting "No Justice… No Peace!" A few were angry blaring their car horns while screaming, "Does anyone know where this little boy resides?" You were given the role as caretaker, one of many unwanted obligations the oldest daughter inherits. But just think what could have happened to your little brother. But because you showed remorse for an impetuous act, your unqualified mis-inherited obligations went without punishment. For Christ's sake you were only eight!

After Daddy was murdered during the Civil Rights Movement, your extended family had to share the responsibilities of nurturing. Up the street was Grandma Jannie and Aunt Eddie Ruth, always baking treats.

Then there was Grandpa Neil who lived on a farm. He planted lots of fresh fruits and vegetables. Mmm come harvest time his grandchildren were the first to eat.

Then there was Papa Davis, who wore a neatly pressed Sears Sucker suit. He knew everything imaginable about trees. He could take down the biggest, with just one push.

And then there was over 30 aunts and just as many uncles.

Last, but not least, the two Mrs. Georgia's. One on the corner and one across the street. They're Momma's right-hand women. Try and leave the neighbourhood if dare. Out of nowhere one would appear yelling "Girl get back here!"

Your family was locked into their law-abiding Godly beliefs. Swore, there is no power higher than almighty God. I'm grateful they were able to provide a holy place to grow and be a happy kid.

Yes, you were rich in Religion and Family. Yet you lacked life's greatest aspect, which no one could replace; your Daddy. He was the only one investing time to teach the fundamentals of life. Everyone else allowed this delicate flower to grow... WILD...

Whoosh! Out of the barn's gates comes WILD you. A naive teenager without Planned Parenthood anticipating that the intrigue and influence of Legbar's kiss would prematurely introduce you to sex.

You became a teenage mother then a wife. Who would have known that I would have a natural aptitude for motherhood...I knew! You grew old and exhausted stumbling unpretentious through life's tricks and turns.

So, you levelled-up on facts, not fiction. You studied irrefragable truth concerning: Ancestors, Slavery, and The Weeping Time; Love, Parenting, and Marriage; Equality, Gender Confusion, and Freedom; Economic; Politics, God, Race, and Religion etc....

Truth unveiled the Church's lies and trapped secrets this Country kept closed. You too learned to accept those lies, infidelity, and abuse...

You were experiencing recurring nightmares of unexplainable horrifying affairs. Your only resolution was to seek Holistic Care. So, you chopped it up with your very reliable hydromancy Potter, and Prof. Pythagoras, who's a realist. Both divulge that your nightmares are the result of hellacious fights you've witnessed between

Mom and Dad when you were an infant. That was the end of your nightmares.

Your Therapists also opened epic visions of curses: past, present, and future regarding your skin; some virtuous memories, and anamnesis of hidden traumas. Mainly, the ones that dismantle you; the murder of Daddy and the flood of 1994.

Hell's disquieting tidal waves pushed foreign change of unmeasurable sizes. Each wave imports Hell's dementors hidden under white sheets carrying communism bloody baggage. Although some were good and some vexed. Overtime both made your old-world feel cursed and extraordinarily complex.

Oppression is your bitter torch to bearerth! You can't help but wonder where was God then?

America has exhibited time and time again your skin is not good enough for some and not pure enough for others. Steady flow of Hell's endless curses pushed Historical Black Neighbourhoods and your American Base back to the Flint River. Leaving your stability only as memories of yester years!

Experiencing the pain and hardships of oppression caused you to slid and lament into darkness. Yet, later in life you've received counselling for depression/anxiety and levelled up on knowledge. But life continues to hurl new tricks and turns.

For years enslavement for exploitation and labouring people with your skin has been America's countless facets of infrastructures used to create this country.

Plus, les choses changent, plus ells restent les mêmes.

Who-so-ever told this undermining lie that things will never change for the good of my people, Never met the out the box disciple that this cruel aegis world groomed you to be.

Revelation has it!

Your oppressors continue to weigh heavy on your freedom. Therefore, your truths must be reframed!

You're never the lesser...

You're a proud American beautiful Black Woman!

Your flames blaze highest!

For in this moment... You're your Elder's Nihilist!

You're one of several diverse existentialist Writers, Poets, Spoken Word Artists, History Realist, and Freedom Activists who's working hard to ensure...

We are FREE!

FREE to Live Happy inside Our Own Skin...

Cynthia Butler Jackson

Be Bold, Be You

Hey you! I want to let you to know something and I hope you take this all in, because it's really important for you to know.

Young lady...I would like to tell you, to really take time to find yourself, get to know what you like and what you don't like, spend time alone and value those moments of reflection. Always be ready to learn something new about yourself... before awakening love in your life! Just make sure, when you're READY to awaken love, know what a good man acts like, looks like, talks like and also understand that, not all men are same. But ALSO importantly, set your boundaries, be firm, but gentle. Trust is earned, so never trust easily, let them prove it, show it and act it, before you are fully convinced of who they are and what their intentions are. Got it? Great!!

When it comes to relationships...ALWAYS RESPECT YOURSELF - Recognise what real love acts like and be bold enough to walk away, if it's not reciprocated. Rejection may hurt and God knows, it can feel like the end of the world, but learn from the red flags, that present themselves right from the start, so you can limit any future pain. But understand and know you can't avoid it altogether, it's part of the human experience to go through challenges and some of those can cause severe pain, so just have a box of tissues at the ready... but this too shall pass eventually and you will be stronger for it.

How you feel about your self is important, so learn to embrace the colour of your skin in all its glory, and ignore those magazines or conversations with men, who want to compare you to others, especially, when they don't even look like you. NEVER change your hair texture, to try to fit in...be comfortable and learn to look after what God gave you, treat it with care and attention, spend money on the best products and lavish your time on it, when it needs doing. Girl, it's beautiful!

Don't be afraid to speak articulately and if your voice confuses others let them be confused, you owe no one an apology for your diction! This does not determine your lack of blackness. You have nothing to prove to anyone, there is always going to be someone who has a problem with it. Just ignore them and continue to speak up. Be BOLD!

As a young woman, learn to embrace your weirdness and don't let others, dampen your personality and your creative streak, it's the essence of who you are. Not everyone will get you, but wait for the ones that do and when they arrive, you will recognise them instantly, so look out for them on your travels.

Remember! To fully trust in the one that knows every single hair on your head, by making the RIGHT CHOICES, that are not influenced by loneliness, because you may feel needy. You will need that spiritual guidance, to not only keep you grounded, but stop you from speaking words that are negative to yourself and thoughts you may have of others. It's just for your protection okay?

Be aware of your strengths and learn to love others, through always being kind, though some may be perplexed by it and will not always know how to react to it. Often some may even treat you with suspicion, because you're nice to them - Not everyone understands your heart. Be okay with that. Don't let it stop you loving on people though!

Be prepared to take more risks in life, by following up on those studies, that you need - your accomplishments in the future, will benefit from it and don't put off from getting some piano/keyboard lessons, you'd always dreamed about and all of those songs you wrote- record them. Listen to your intuition, find your musical tribe early, and go to those live music events and outdoor festivals, where jazz plays in the wind and the summer sun, glistens and lightly tans your skin. When it comes to your health, get used to regular physical exercise and make it part of your lifestyle, you know how that makes you feel right? Drink more water and always eat a well-balanced diet too, don't forget to take advantage of body and foot massages for your well-being, it will also help your stress levels, and keep them at bay.

Again, when it comes to those human relationships, try your best to forgive others, when they wrong you or are insensitive to your needs. Recognise that the problem was NEVER YOU…it was always about them. Remember, when you're feeling misunderstood and isolated, find your happy place and stay there until the feeling has passed. You are a wonderful, sensitive human being, with a heart full of love and always willing to support others and that will never change. So always affirm yourself daily and in particular, when you may be feeling down or someone has upset you, keep reminding yourself, you are beautifully and wonderfully made, but are also fragile and sensitive – very human and it's okay to be disappointed sometimes. You will learn from it.

Enjoy being you, love on yourself more, reminding yourself of the woman you would like to become, by surrounding yourself with exceptionally positive and creative people, who will inspire you. It's okay to handle yourself with kid gloves and try to avoid taking yourself too seriously. Relax and embrace the opportunity to explore the world with different eyes, to the ones that others want to see you through.-They, my friend are too myopic for you (lol)

Please…please, DON'T FORGET to take time to plan small trips or go abroad, as often as you can afford to. Try that solo travelling, so you can meet others, just like you, which would be great right? You will learn so much about history, when you explore other cultures, their food, books, and music and you will discover so much about yourself in that time too. Embrace it all, it will be so much fun for you!

Visit those places where art resides, the museums, take an art class, and learn a new language. Read more books.

Girl, and remember, you better stick to people, that bring laughter into your life and don't forget to keep in touch with those, that have loved on you and care about you. BE prepared to live life to the fullest, enjoy those crushes, and understand they will come and go. It's just a sign that you are a young woman that, feels, is wonderfully alive and open to expressing her feelings, even if you never ever speak to your crush in the end. You'll learn that its healthy and not at all embarrassing. Still, if you get asked out to dinner or for a walk in the park...go on those dates, treat it like a bit of fun, relax and enjoy!

When it comes to your finances, spend that money on expensive items, every few months. Regularly pamper yourself and get your nails and feet done, you will feel so much better for doing it. However, DO save more, but be frugal, when you need to be, but don't be too stingy with yourself.

One other thing you need to remember, learn to drive, take those lessons don't let no one put you off from doing so! Just picture yourself driving with the roof down, music playing along beautiful scenic routes, while nature continues to happen all around you. Visualise that regularly.

Lastly....when you look in that mirror, know that everything you will ever need to know, comes with wisdom, failure, and heart break! But you will get through it, it will make you stronger, although it may not feel like that at the time, but it will.

Learn to laugh in the rain, give more hugs, and only say 'I LOVE YOU', when you really, UNDERSTAND what it means. Never let ANYONE stop you from being YOU! And if they do, then they are not meant for you or don't need to be a part of your life!

I love you big time, so make sure you love you too.

Big Hugs
ME x

H.P.

A Life Of Passion

Dear Younger Self,

Life has many wonders ahead for you… It is like a box of chocolates, so much to choose from, but all you have to do is keep your eyes open, keep your eyes on the prize, and seize every moment, and if you look carefully there are many wonderful moments to come.

Some sayings and rules that have served me well so far include: - Live like there's no tomorrow, (because you don't know that there will be one), Love like you've never been hurt, (believe me you will be), and dance like there's no one watching, (you can't live your life worrying about what others will say).

People don't remember you for what you say, they remember you for how you make them feel…Maya Angelou (So where and when possible be kind).

Don't expect the same standard of others that you have, you could be disappointed. At 17, you know you will not believe it but "life is short" so, be ambitious, be curious, grow your resilience, you will need it, be passionate, be confident, you will only be hurt by others, if you let them hurt you, others will only bring you joy if you let them, be fearless and focus on your focus. If you follow those rules you will never be bored, have enough time to do all the things you want to, meet all the amazing people you might like to, and get to all the places on your wish list.

"Reciprocity Rocks," always give back, because karma can be a bitch, better still pay it forward.

Since the advent of the internet, the world is now at your fingertips. Make use of it. If you knew then what you know now, you will have lived a fruitful life. A life with passion that wakes you up in the morning and passion that keeps you up at night. You will be so passionate about life, that sleep will get in the way.

This is for you because, yesterday is now the past, tomorrow is the future but today is a gift that's why its call a present.

Use each second like a heartbeat, use it wisely, use it with love, because like time you don't know when it may just stop!

Don't forget Be kind and love yourself, and others. I wish I had an older self, handing me down these guidelines to life.

Your always – Older and Wiser

Dr Yvonne Thompson CBE

Pause, Breathe and Enjoy

Hi there, from your older version here.

I'm now over 40 years old. I was in your place, as my younger self not so long ago. Born in Zambia a country in the centre of Southern Africa, landlocked with no sea line except other countries surrounding the country. I travelled to England an Island in Europe. I found myself here, as a teenager for what is commonly known as greener pastures, the land of plenty opportunity and growth, so everyone around me said.

I thought, I must get me to this glorious land of opportunity. Here, my story and experiences lie.

I'm delighted to look back, reflect and pull up some tips that would have made my journey thus far a little less bumpy; still, it's with great joy that I step forward, look back and write this letter to you. I hope with this, your journey will be less bumpy, a little more cushioned. Now sit back and enjoy the read. Believe me when I say to you that I understand how you feel.

The thoughts that ponder your mind, your secret fears and desires.

My advice to you is to be able to pause, breath, enjoy your journey through.

The ups and downs, everyone faces. Different they may present yet the emotions and energy expressed so similar; don't believe those that seem to have It all together, even they sometimes experience the insecurities, the same fears and desires you too are experiencing.

They sooner you learn to take care of yourself, mentally, physically, spiritually and emotionally, the more balanced you will become, with the ability to quickly bounce back from difficult experiences and moments.

Accept yourself, accept who you are, where you come from and where you are now. Create in your mind a vision of what you want out of life, but don't let it consume you; live, love and laugh along the way. You are fine and perfect just as you are, created and crafted by the master himself in his own very image; beautiful, wonderful, fearfully made, you are a master piece.

Remember don't be afraid to be bold, brave and pursue your ambition; you can be whatever you want, you can do all things through Christ who strengthens you.

Take one step at a time, moving forward with confidence, in faith, every good desire is from God and where there is a will there always is a way. Don't pursue money, as you will find many do, rather pursue service, serve others by being a solution to others. Your solution will make you master of your service and as you serve money will follow.

Don't waste your time pursuing everything, don't be jack of all trade be a master of one thing, become the very best of that one thing so that everyone knows to come to you first in that field. I learnt this lesson rather a bit late, but it's a game changer if you master it sooner.

Always know your worth, be kind to yourself, take time to look after your wellbeing.

Don't waste your time worrying, do your best be authentic, enjoy being you and trust in God.

You are well worth it.

With love,

Priscilla Muyunda, your older version

Stay Strong

Dear Rachel,

You are loved beyond your imagination. No one understands what you're going through, and that must be difficult. Know that you are supported by your family and by forces far greater than any earthly experience.

You are a precious part of Divine Creation and you are never alone. The Universe has your back. Trust your gut, believe in yourself and take steps towards your dreams and goals. Even when things seem to crumble, remember that there is always light at the end of the tunnel, and rain truly does make the flowers grow.

Don't sweat the small stuff - it's not worth it. Don't worry - you will be cared for and looked after your entire life. Make time to take good care of yourself - you can't pour from an empty cup.

Find the beauty in the present moment, and listen to your heart. Your gifts are yours alone, while at the same time meant to be shared to uplift humanity. You have the power to make choices that honour yourself and your mental well-being before anything else.

Write your own story. Cherish each moment and love deeply, for time is an illusion and there is nothing but the present. Shine your light to the world and soon you'll see that the world loves you back. Stay strong, young Rachel. Life gets better. I promise. You are destined for greatness.

Love,

44-year-old Rachel

You Will Never Lose Your Self

Dear 17-year-old Me,

You are about to go into the living room and with a tremor in your voice to ask your parents how they would feel if you told them you had a boyfriend and that he wasn't Bosnian like them.

Things will not go well. You already know that going in, but trust me, they will really not go well. There is no advice I can give you today on how to go about it so that things might go better because the truth is, they would react how they did no matter how you told them. This isn't about them, it's about you. And in a way, that is the advice. Don't waste your time on trying to control what other people do, because you can't.

Though their reaction will be extreme, take heart, my darling. You are doing a good thing and a brave thing. Above all, you are doing the right thing. You do indeed deserve recognition for yourself and your relationship. It will hurt that they won't be able to find it in themselves to support you and be happy for you, but that is their failing, not yours. And they're very possibly bluffing, you know. It won't feel like it because they will say things so harsh you will feel your heart breaking into a hundred pieces, but don't take it entirely seriously. If there is one piece of advice I can give you from now, over 20 years later, it's that. They will try to scare you into toeing the line and it is about to backfire horribly on them. They are about to lose a daughter thanks to their callousness.

You will be OK. Even though things will never heal between you and your family, regardless of how much energy you will put into it over the next ten years, and even though you will slowly lose your entire community because of that, know this: You will be OK because even though you will lose them, you will never lose yourself. You will do well. You will even go settle in a whole new country entirely on your own because you are unstoppable. You will have success and freedom and independence. It will be at a high price, considering you didn't do anything wrong. Facing the world alone isn't easy, I won't lie. But sometimes in life, you get punished without having done anything wrong. Just know that you can handle it.

You will not be alone for long. You will build a wonderful new community for yourself -- and yes, it will include other Bosnians who, like you, will know that love is love. Family is what you make for yourself, dear 17-year-old me. Be generous with your friends, be devoted to them -- and this is very important: Make sure they know you are there for them. They are the ones who will be with you through thick and thin. You will travel far and on your own and you will make friends everywhere. Hold on to them. That will be your tribe and it will be even bigger and kinder than the one you're about to lose today. They will be your kind of people, they will share in your joys and losses, and they will open up the world to you as you will open up the world to them.

Though I know you would have preferred to have been older when you lost your family and though I would have preferred it for you, know that you are already strong and will only get stronger. You can do things and withstand things you cannot even fathom. Even if it right now feels like you need a safety net and like you need your mummy and daddy, I can tell you that you don't. They would have been nice to have, yes, but you do not need them. You do not rely on them. You are taking care of yourself already, sweetheart, you are standing up for yourself and you will continue to do so. Your sense of right and wrong is spot on, and you know your gut feeling well. Stick to that and you will be alright because you will never lose your way.

Please don't get hung up on what you're losing today. It's their loss, my love, not yours. They will miss out on all the wonderful things you are and will do.

Do not doubt that you are capable. If anyone tries to tell you otherwise, it is because they are trying to plant that seed of self-doubt in your mind. Don't fall for it, my darling. They are only afraid of what you can do when you put your mind to it. It may be a cliché, but you would not believe how much fear a strong, independent woman still evokes in some people. You have no time for that. You are too busy being awesome.

Now, go into that living room and do your thing, however you choose to do it knowing what you know now -- with that tremor still in your voice or without it. You are carving your own path today. In fact, you have already been carving it for quite some time. However the chips fall, you own that. You are in charge. And I could not be prouder of you.

Amila Jašarević

Just The Way You're Supposed To Be

Dear Natalie,

You are an exceptional, talented and clever girl who has so much potential. If only you could believe that you are enough.

You have to believe that you have been perfectly made and don't take to heart what others say or do to you because it's just a reflection of them. Be careful not to absorb that negative energy because it will consume you.

It's absolutely fine to ask for help. Don't be afraid of rejection because that thing that you thought you longed for wasn't meant for you. God only placed it in your vision so you'd understand the lesson. Honey, there's so much people rooting for you, and my dear, they've already envisioned your success! You are powerful and influential beyond belief and you need to recognise this as early as possible.

It's okay to let go. But let go quickly and recognise that the actions and behaviour of these boyfriends, friends and your dad are displayed to teach you about loyalty and trust, as well as to toughen you up! Learn to follow your intuition more often and walk away from work, friends' men and situations that no longer serve you. You have to find your voice and use it so you can protect your sanity and heart.

Don't ever let anyone tell you that you are not enough or not beautifully created. If only I could go back in time to give you the extra cuddles and praise that you needed because I know it would have made you more confident and boosted your self-esteem.

Please don't judge yourself based on others around you. You are a different, special person that has special powers and it does make some people feel somewhat intimidated and uncomfortable; that's no concern of yours.

You are adventurous and that's okay to take more intended risks. I know you're sensible and calculated so aim for the moon!

Speak up and speak out. Don't be afraid to shine or stand up for yourself, even if no-one sees your point of view at first. Practise this early on and it will build your self-esteem and authority.

As for your hair – it is perfect in every way. God created you in his vision. You don't need to look like everyone else and that's okay. Afro hair is the best!

Please take time out to rest, recuperate and reflect. Master the art of being more focused and disciplined as it will help you in the long run.

You're brilliant at saving and giving but you can't save the world so be more mindful of who you help! I'd strongly encourage you to concentrate on investing your finances and buy that property like you always wanted.

'Don't worry Natty' as your Grandma would say. And she was right! Practise loving and praising yourself more. You will find that partner who loves you for exactly you at the right time. You will kiss lots of frogs, but don't compromise and settle out of frustration and desperation. You deserve only the best and will get what you deserve.

There is nothing wrong with your body. You are not a sexual object defined by your breasts. Your beautifully curvy and feminine body was specially created for you, your partner and child so value your body, beauty and health because you only get one.

Remember God gave you a special gift of talking and connecting with people because you are a brilliant communicator. It will carry you far.

Everything will work out for you, just the way as it supposed to!

I love you, value you and see the potential in you. You are enough and always have been. Sit up, stand tall, walk straight and with your head held high.

Natalie Joseph

The Heart To Heart

It's been a long time since we have had a heart to heart beautiful woman.

One of the things that was never discussed when you were growing up was sex and maybe just maybe if it were, you would have realised just how Sacred the act of 2 becoming 1 is and you wouldn't have exposed your inner self so frivolously. When you were a young girl you were exposed to sexual images via pornographic magazines that you found under your mama's mattress; that was over 3 decades ago and my oh my what a journey you have been on since then.

My dear child the womb is sacred, all powerful; the seat of sexuality, creativity, fertility and rebirth for a woman. I came across a quote which read "therefore once you believe this and know this you cannot allow an unqualified man in". I'm sure that was meant with no disrespect to men but the point I am trying to get across to you is that it would have been far better for you to save yourself until the divine time than to allow for the flesh to lead you into a life of lustfulness, emotionless sex.

This cycle of meaningless sex continued for you for decades and the men just wouldn't stop cumming, excuse the pun. When you got older and realised that sex alone didn't cut it you were still caught lying there like a corpse letting men have their wicked way with you because you wouldn't speak up.

I've only ever wanted the best for you my dear child. I didn't want you to think that your beauty was a tool for you to allow men to use. You didn't know that when you meet a guy you could hold off from having sex and just get to know each other and because of that you allowed them into your walls of love, thinking that they loved you even though you knew deep down that love was not part of the equation.

You learnt the lesson late and ended up feeling like the rotten core of an apple left on the kitchen counter after several bites had been taken. You even lost a fallopian tube after travelling 10 miles for a 1 night stand where you went through an uncomfortable ordeal of being twisted, bent and spread for hours; leaving the following morning bruised finding yourself six weeks later on an operating table having a salpingectomy as a result of an ectopic pregnancy.

The elders always used to say "when you don't hear you must feel." I don't know why, but you went so far with your rebellion to feel as if you didn't believe what your granny was telling you. 1 miscarriage, 2 ectopics and 2 terminations; enough was enough. God intervened and spoke to you through the anaesthetist who before putting you to sleep politely said "I don't ever want to see you on this operating table again". Thank God you were wonderfully created and thank God for his Grace and his mercies which resulted in you being able to bore a child years later.

I remember you sitting in your grandmother's room every Sunday morning whilst she made you read 2 lines of scripture before passing the bible around. I wish when you were of age that your Grandma would have explained 1st Corinthians 6 to you:

'Flee from sexual immorality. All other sins a man commits are outside his body, but he who sins sexually sins against his own body.
Do you not know that your body is a temple of the Holy Spirit, who is in you, whom you have received from God? You are not your own; you were bought at a price. Therefore honour God with your body.'

It took the best part of 30 years for you to realise that you weren't loving yourself. You placed others needs above your own and even though you told yourself that you loved yourself deep down you questioned that. In spite of all you endured and all you put yourself through, you freed yourself from the entanglement and entrapments of casual sex realising that you are worth so much more.

J.L.B

Trauma That Travels

Dear Willel,

I'm writing this to you, from the dim and distant future. First of all, well done for surviving this far; you've made it to sixty-two! From where I am now, I can see you in your various manifestations of trauma and my heart aches for you. There's so much that you don't understand.

First let me acknowledge that leaving Dominica as a toddler for the U.K. (with that strange woman they said was our mother) was terrifying. There's so much trauma even in that one sentence. We left behind the love of our grandparents, freedom to play and everything that was light, colourful and warm, to journey thousands of miles to a cold, drab, dirty and hostile place. No wonder that left a scar; a wound so deep that even now, more than sixty years later, the wound still seeps, unable to heal. No one knew the suffering of that small girl, when she was told year after year that 'next year we would go home.' Only to realise at age seven, that she was being fobbed off and that we were never going home.

Being a mother myself now I can understand why you acted out your distress and became known as a difficult child. They didn't understand the distress they were causing. How could our parents have known that false promises of our imminent return to Dominica would be so damaging? How could they have known that the disappointment and grief that it created would fester into this well of rage and resentment towards them? Even now, I still feel the rage and grief at being lied to and for never seeing our beloved grandparents again before they died.

The experience of settling from one part of the British Empire to another, has taught me a very valuable lesson that I want to share with you. While as a seven-year-old child we struggled to comprehend the enormity of the knowledge that parents can lie, it led to the much later understanding that parents try to do the best for their children and most parents just don't have all the equipment they need to do the job. Nowadays, there are external resources that parents can call upon when they realise that there is something that they cannot handle themselves, but back in our childhood, there was practically nothing.

I put myself in their shoes and I can only feel compassion and love, for they too were traumatised. We only saw a small part of what they endured. They shielded us from the worst of it and taught us about our own culture so we had a haven, a little Dominica to return to every day, a place of language, meals, stories, family and good friends. Unbeknownst to them, they kept a channel of communication open with Mother Africa, by teaching us these cultural practices it gave us a link to our Mother and it kept the hostile world out. This was very important to us and it is another valuable lesson. Make sure that our children know and love their Dominican culture.

In my maturity, I have come to realise that many of our generation were also wounded this way. Only now can I see the significance of our experiences and the importance of sharing our stories. People need to hear them and today I am out there making sure that they listen. You and I are making our mark.

Yes, life was hard for us. After a life free from restrictions in Dominica, in comparison, living conditions in London were terrible. How can anyone not compare them negatively? Tenement housing, being exposed to prostitution (yes, I remember the lady downstairs and understand now why Mamma was always so tight-lipped), overt racism and criminal landlords. Our little girl self was such a fun-loving child that even in those moments when it seemed that the sun had forgotten this wind-blasted and godforsaken island, she and her little Irish cohort would dash off to play on the cleared bombsite across the road or on that British Rail wasteland that was their playground.

Those episodes where her imagination took over and allowed her to play, were what saved her. Being able to retreat into her imagination created a safe haven for her. That same spirit of fun that we developed in childhood will sustain you, nurture it and don't let anyone grind you down. Don't ever let that passion for adventure be diminished. It's at the heart of who you are; look inwards for your strength, you'll find it there. Feed it with love and creativity. Keep up with your writing – do you remember Mrs Bose, one of your teachers at St Mary's? She was right, you are a writer.

No matter what, always make time for your writing. You are a Creative, so create. You come from a family of Creatives. There was an understanding back then that Black kids aren't creative, that's BS. Go over, under, around, even through obstacles if you have to. Don't believe such rubbish. You don't know where your creativity might take you. Continue to play the recorder (it's a beautiful instrument so don't let anyone mock you), learn other instruments when you can.

Above all, reconnect with Mother Africa; your spirit resides there with your Ancestors. Those out-of-body experiences you have? They are your clue. Your spirit travels, trust it. Learn practices that will strengthen your bond with the Ancestors. The sooner you learn the better it will be for you. You don't know how many other people this will benefit. Your Ancestors will guide your footsteps; trust them for the good of your health – physical, spiritual, psychological, and emotional.

The experiences throughout your childhood and teenage years that left you raging inwardly, feeling powerless and feeling that you have no voice will continue into adulthood. That is the experience of many young black women of your generation. So be warned, there is more to come. Steel yourself, know now that you are not alone. Once you make that connection with the Ancestors, they will support you in all you do. So although some things may seem overwhelming and random at the time, even these negative experiences can be harnessed and put to good use, they will motivate and drive you later on. The people who abuse, torment and insult you have no idea what they are unleashing on the world. This slow flowing lava will consume all future BS in its path. You can control it through your narrative. Let it be the ink that flows from your pen.

Let go of the rage, girl. Don't let it poison your relationship with Mamma. Daddy's gone; killed by toxic exhaustion and Mamma is all we have left. Encourage her to grow her creativity for she is the key to our own. Hold her up for the Queen that she is. Recognise that she is a human being first, imperfect as are all human beings. Observe this wonderful, warm, funny lady with new eyes, for by doing so, you will begin to understand so much more about yourself. Unravel your narrative, see how it has shaped your journey. Accept what cannot be changed. Look where this path has brought you and let it be your power. Never let good fuel go to waste.

With love from your future self,

Willelmina Joseph-Loewenthal

The Older You Get, The Better It Gets

Hello you!

It's not often people get letters from their older self and so hopefully this will help you understand not to take everything to heart and concentrate on moving forward with your life's journey and purpose.

When you were born Ruth, your older brother of 5 years old, couldn't help but torment you. His jealousy of your mere existence, which had knocked him off his "only child" perch, took over his every thought, making it difficult for him to be kind to you which in turn made it extremely difficult for you two to have a close relationship. Thankfully, you are strong and thoughtful and will find a way to overcome this in later life.

Your outgoing personality comes from your father and luckily for you, you are two peas out of the same pod, which you will not fully appreciate until a few years after he has passed on. They say, when your parents have passed on, they live inside of you and being as close as you are to your father, you will notice where you get your zany mannerisms and comedic sense of humour from. We are all blessed with gifts and talents and it is such a pleasure to see you pursuing your dreams, with your love of music. I am so impressed to see that with every career decision you are making, it is bringing you new experiences and new people into your life.

You recognise the opportunities when they come and you step into them. Know that as long as these opportunities make you feel good then you will always be going in the right direction. If there is a trace of negative feeling in a venture, then don't pursue it. I always say, what's for you will not go by you

I learned this saying halfway through my life and have often referred to it over the years. Sometimes I ask myself, " why hadn't I done such and such, all those years ago, but life has its own journey and way of working out the details. No one could have predicted that you would go to university in your 30's and come out with a wonderful 2:1 honours degree when you couldn't wait to leave school before your 16th birthday.

Always try to put yourself in the right environment for your talents to blossom and grow. Find your tribe no matter how long it takes. Follow people who inspire you and aspire to be like them. Don't waste time trying to fit in. Life is going to throw you some curve balls and they are going to upset you.

Learn to confide in people and don't try to bottle up all your thoughts and feelings. Be who you are and not who you think that you should be. You will not have straight romantic relationships and you will have to be brave and courageous in facing up to your identity in the world. You are growing up in a world where it is not cool to be in a gay relationship. How can I make you believe that one day, marriage will be an option for you and there's a wonderful woman you will eventually fall in love with. You will learn how to have deep, honest, meaningful relationships and this will set you free to be who you are meant to be.

You will see, that the older you get, the better it gets......

Ruth Franks

Batten Down And Enjoy The Ride

Dear Ingrid,

Being born towards the end of WW2, you were not aware of life before bleak austerity, clothing and food rationing, a family mainly of women and the odd elderly uncle, young menfolk visiting occasionally in uniform, on leave, and so you accepted what could have been seen as hardships as normal. Your father was in Intelligence, based in Malta, intercepting and translating enemy messages, and wasn't demobbed until you were 2 years old, until when you had thought that "daddy" was the little gold locket that your mother wore around her neck (that contained a photo of a handsome Air Force Officer), because she was used to saying to you, "Look, darling. This is your daddy!"

You were so fortunate to have the parents you did. They were so in love with each other, so honest and relaxed in each other's company. At one stage, when you were young, fancy free, and playing the dating game, it was somewhat of a handicap, because you weren't prepared to settle for a "good enough" feeling, an "it'll do" relationship, and disconcerted your mother by turning down a few proposals from really lovely boyfriends because you knew that you didn't feel that "love forever" feeling. Remember how stunned your mother was when, after just one date with Nick, you came home and said, "I've met the man I'm going to marry!"

You always will be a bolshie character, sticking up for what you believe in rather than sacrificing your principles in order to fit in with a group, locking antlers and relishing debate in order to sway others to your point of view. That trait will stand you in good stead over the years.

You shouldn't ever imagine compromising on the things that truly matter to you. Over the years, you will nurture your friendships, some for over seventy years and, although you don't realise it now, you are lucky that these folk stay around with you, laughing with you, sharing your triumphs, and supporting you on the occasions when grief struck you down, always holding your history for you in their loving hands.

You will tend your career enthusiastically, always working hard to be the best you can be, not for plaudits, just simply for the satisfaction of a job well done. You understood that you were to spend a large proportion of your life at work, and so it was necessary to enjoy it by choosing a profession that gave you meaning and rewarded you with the knowledge that you were making a difference to people's lives. Your work will open doors that enable you to connect with people from all walks of life, from billionaires to those living on the breadline without money to spare and who needed your generosity. You will see beauty in most all of them, and watch them thrive as you accompany them momentarily along their lives' paths.

You will have, for the most part, a charmed life full of love, if not necessarily a financially wealthy one. You will always have enough to provide you and those you love with a comfortable home and food on your table, enough to spare. The magical people that you need to learn from along the way will appear and share their wisdom. Always trust the universe, because it is bountiful. As you grow old and more familiar with the passing of loved ones, hold to your heart the memories of the fun and joy in closeness with them, and remember that love never dies. Always remember to trust people until proved otherwise, because everyone does the best they can. Sometimes people have hard lessons to learn in their lives, and are unable to contain their hurt and despair. Don't take it personally if sometimes you become collateral damage.

Above all, understand and appreciate what a privilege it is to be alive and to be able to love. Remember that happiness is your birthright and it multiplies by sharing. Now batten down the hatches and enjoy the ride!

Ingrid Collins

Don't Dilute Your Attributes

My Dear Younger Self

So, you want to be liked, to fit in and be a part of the social crowd you hang out with, or even feel more connected with your kith and kin in your new abode in the strange and more liberated society you have migrated to, six thousand miles from home. At the tender age of eighteen who can blame you? Who wouldn't? Coming from a very large and very warm and loving family of ten children, you are naturally extremely homesick and prone to suffer from loneliness.

But having a drink with the others is not the way to go about it. After all, you absolutely abhor the thought of women imbibing alcohol, that is grown men's pastime. That is a belief your dear mother passed on to your young mind and which you accepted as a given.

You have a very strong moral ethic instilled in you by your parents from inception and by your loving and closely-knit family, and also by the strong and caring community you grew up in your motherland, the beautiful land called Zimbabwe in Southern Africa. Now, at the tender age of eighteen, you have come to pastures new, to live in the diaspora, in multicultural though cold England, in the United Kingdom, to further your studies and explore new horizons. It is September 1979.

Soon my dear Younger Self you discover that drink is a big part of all social gatherings in your new home. Where two or more are gathered, that is the common language that connects them all.

It is indeed drink that reduces your shyness, hence loosening your inhibitions and help you to speak your mind and also "speak the same language" as your peers, so to speak.

This you interpret as being more accepted by and loved, part of the crowd of your fun-loving peers and family members who you look up to. In this far away land where you sometimes feel very lonely and lost and so very homesick, you have to have crutches to keep you sane. But my dear Younger Self, it is quite ok to be yourself, to not follow the crowd but be your own strong person that God created you to be "fearfully and wonderfully made" in His image.

In your innocence and naivety, you are not to know of the possible dangers that alcohol can potentially pose to your health, if taken regularly and in excess. That you will learn much later on in life, mainly through witnessing others whose lives are to be destroyed by the hazardous liquid pleasures. Youth is a time in our life when consequences are very far away from our pleasure-seeking and still developing minds. For now, you are having fun, but believe me that short-lived fun can turn to misery later if not sooner. For apart from its other harm on health, regular consumption of alcohol, just like a junk food diet, is laden with empty calories often leading to unwanted weight gain. Sadly, it really can be a case of, "A moment on your lips, a lifetime on your hips!"

So my dear Younger Self, you do not yet know this, but your internal organs, that is your liver, your heart, your kidneys, your stomach and the whole digestive system, your brain and the whole nervous system, your reproductive organs and also, even your eyes can be affected by regular heavy drinking, should that be your chosen lifestyle.

Our wonderful body organs, as the Creator made them, and efficient systems are amazingly inter-linked and work in a domino-effect manner. What affects one organ or system can ultimately affect a more remote and seemingly unconnected organ or system of this magnificent network.

You may not know it yet my dear Younger Self, but your mental, emotional and spiritual health are heavily governed by your lifestyle choices. So if those choices are unwise, you can unwittingly set yourself up for bigger challenges later on in your precious life.

The natural course of your life can potentially be changed forever, should you choose the 'pleasure' of regular, heavy drinking.

So, after your night of great fun, you have to face a whole day at work where you need all your focus and attention, energy and patience but these skills can be in short supply the morning after the day before.

You may be distracted and unfocused, tired and lethargic, irritable and impatient with others and yourself. That, my dear Younger Self can potentially affect your work place and general relationships.

However, your naturally good manners and respect of others may buffer your possible poor performance resulting from potential over-indulgence.

Being a perfectionist by nature, underperformance is unacceptable to you and thus incurring a hangover, apart from its physical discomfort, can result in feelings of failure and dissatisfaction with your life. This my dear Younger Self, may lower your self-esteem and self-confidence.

It is by God's grace you may avoid major damage to your health and wellbeing even if your chosen lifestyle may displease Him.

Your loving, God-fearing and strict upbringing bestowed in you a very strong God-given moral code that ensures any potential loss of inhibition is well contained. You have well-defined values that you try hard to adhere to.

As they rightfully say, it takes a whole village to raise child. So too has that applied to you, and in your case, the village has produced a lovable, honest and an obedient child indeed.

Your love, in intimacy, always comes from your heart, soul and your head. You may witness others around you losing their morals along with the loosened inhibitions, and indeed may have to fight off unwanted attention and over-familiarity. Even with God, good luck and maybe even as well, your loving and ever watchful departed ancestors, always watching over you, always on your side and protecting you, you have to do your bit to avoid and minimise danger to yourself. That, my dear Younger Self, is your sole responsibility. Even God needs our helping hand sometimes, since He gave us the gift of free will.

You may seem to wander away from Mwari, Musikavanhu or God, your wonderful Creator, but your faith in His existence remains discreetly intact.

Sunday shifts at work and late nights of fun on Saturdays may limit your regular church attendance, but deep, deep down in your heart you never stray from His love and guidance.

If you are unfortunate enough to develop the drinking habit, and you may not know it until it is too late my dear Younger Self, you may find drink being the first comfort and uplifter of spirits you go to in most situations you will face in life, happy or sad.

It can easily turn to this vicious cycle; something makes you happy -> have a drink, someone upsets you at home -> drink, your partner upsets you -> drink, someone upsets you at work -> drink, children misbehave -> drink, someone upsets you at church -> drink, you feel overwhelmed -> drink, someone upsets you in your extended family -> drink, someone got happy news -> drink, someone got sad news -> drink, a baby is born - > drink, someone lets you down -> drink, someone dies -> drink the pain away, it is a sunny day -> drink to it, it is a gloomy day - > drink to chase the blues away, a neighbour's cat dies -> drink, and so on and on it can go. Any excuse to imbibe you may justify as a good reason to do so.

And so it can quite easily become a habit, albeit a potentially damaging one before you realise it my dear Younger Self.

You may find yourself drinking to cheer up, to chase the blues away, to celebrate to just feel happier or better ... or so you believe. However, the truth is the 'high' is only short-lived and the 'lows' longer-lasting. Today's upbeat mood may sadly become tomorrow's depression.

Is it not therefore wise to steer away from trouble now, before both your body and mind become accustomed to a potentially toxic habit?

So, my dearest, beloved Younger Self, do you really want to, through possibly over-imbibing in alcohol, risk losing or diluting those great God-given and nurture-instilled gifts, talents, values and enviable attributes bestowed upon and entrusted to you, some already evident and those promised and yet to evolve, all of which make you the Unique You?

These attributes you can continue to Do, Be and Have, and which the Universe has in store for you are:

Mannered	Moralistic	Meticulous
Artistic	Articulate	Approachable
Radiant	Realistic	Reasonable
Imaginative	Influential	Incorruptible
Gifted	Gracious	Generous
Open-minded	Optimistic	Organised
Loving	Lovable	Listener
Determined	Discerning	Dedicated

So, think again my dear Younger Self. Tell me now, my dear Younger Self, would you happily eat monkey, snake, crocodile or chameleon just because 'others' are doing so, even though it is taboo to you and goes against your core, cherished beliefs, values and preferences? Indeed, one man's meat is another's poison. That is the status quo my dear.

Go on my dearest, dare to be bold enough to be true to Yourself. Resist all that temptation, peer pressure and the desire to want to fit in. Dare to believe that you will still be loved, valued and accepted by those who matter in your life, even if you are teetotal or only ever indulge in a very occasional celebratory drink, as your heart is dictating to you. Follow your heart, please my beloved.

Your eternally loving
Older Self <3 <3 <3

P.S: You can always count on me whenever you need my wisdom, guidance and non-judgemental, empathetic and compassionate advice. I have shared your journey and I promise to be available to you 24/7 My Precious Younger Self. Take good care of your Unique, Genius and Irreplaceable self.

Your eternally loving
Older Self <3 <3 <3

Marigold Ndicho Katsande

Fear Not

Dearest Verona,

I have so much to tell you. You are not yet aware of the wonderful journey that lies ahead for you but you are an amazing person and a very gifted one. Life has lots in store for you and you are going to grow in strength and wisdom every day. You will love and you will cry, you will laugh and all your joy and happiness will be eternal ones so never fear, God is with you always.

When you are 4 and a half years old, your mother will leave you with your grandmother for 4 years and those years will be very challenging but embrace them, they are full of precious gifts and contentment that will later be disrupted. The time with your grandmother will be hard as you will need to grow up pretty fast and you will have to deal with some difficult moments which will cause you to wonder why. You will at times feel burdened, but you will overcome with peace and contentment, the love of your little friends and the bond with your brother will bring you joy, so hold on to those memories and remember that you are a child of God and you are in his hand.

When you are 9 years old, you will fly for the first time and wow the excitement you will feel will not really prepare you for what is to come but you will fly with anxious dismay and a great deal of apprehension and weariness as you see your mother again for the first time. All your memories of her will be misty and blurred and the attachment of your early life will be a distant memory that will seem as two strangers meeting for the first time and as usual the thought of your father has not entered the reunion as he continues to be an awareness, not in flesh, but he exists in the background all the same. My advice to you is to embrace the moment, and even when the harsh, snowy weather starts, and you start to lose your lovely thick long and beautiful black hair.

When your fingers sting and burn and jack frost sets in to make you yearn for the familiar happy and challenging warmth of the care free playground with friends that are now beyond the sea, just look forward and remember that the difficulties and the challenges you left behind have prepared you well to overcome and God has you in his hand.

You will go to school to learn, the journey will be hard, but it will develop you and your skills, so never be afraid, confront it. When you fall in love with the beautiful, white, fluffy, ice-cold and deceptive covering on the ground that seems to bring joy and laughter to your pears around you, as they collect and roll the white fluff into balls and play, but yet it only seems to cut into your fingers like an enemy wronged, just remember the pain you feel will strengthen you for warmer days.

The thick dark smog may render you blind but nothing will bring you as much pain as the cutting words and harsh attack brought to bear and delivered by those you have been taught to revere. Adults, that we see as teachers, exemplars and nurturers will present in their delivery to you the enormous monster now known as racism and abuse, but never fear, you are learning and you will take a path that will triumph as each and every experience delivered by their hands is a treasure of wisdom learnt that will empower you for your future life, and for the generation of greatness you will birth and grow in the future; just remember God's hand is in the midst.

You are now eleven going twelve, mother worked around the clock, bought the house after overcoming fathers hinderance to success, his abuse and infidelity. Mother continues to work around the clock. She collapsed and in no time, she was back working around the clock, father was still an essence in the background only emerging occasionally to make demands and make his unfamiliar discipline known. Mother working around the clock, leaving you to manage the home and watch over your younger brothers may have seemed unfair. At times it may seem as though you were caged and had no life, especially when your friends and brothers seem to have life easy; being able to go out and have fun while you wash, cook, clean and would get into trouble if your brothers got up to mischief.

What I want to say to you is; you must see these feelings as a blessing, you will learn great life lessons, you will understand the world better, you will grow to serve, love unconditionally, and find skills in you that you would not have been aware of without your unique and developmental journey. You will grow into a great daughter, sister, aunt, mother and grandmother and you will love all these roles in your life. You will gain great life skills, wisdom and knowledge beyond the average and you will use them to motivate, uplift and empower others in their lives which will bring you joy. Your experience will qualify you in so many ways providing you with more than an academic degree but more effectively a degree of life. God has blessed you well.

As a teenager, at 16yrs old you begin exhorting your need for independence. You have chosen to leave school against all the advice of the adults in your life, but you will do well, although you have learnt from a young age how to mother your brothers, look after the home, learn how to be a home based machinist to help mother, you will come to realise that these skills will later provide you with good strength and mental health when you become a mother in your own right and you will fully appreciate them. Just remember to rise above the mothering role you were conditioned into and let your light shine through. Take time for you, take time to let your light be bright, nurture yourself never let your light go dim, because you do matter and you will bless other lives.

At 17 you will meet your first husband and the father of your first 3 children, even though he is a good man at heart, and had many great qualities, his mental and emotional issues will cause him to let you down and you will love again. You will have 3 further children with your second husband who will be so different to your first and he will fail you and your children in such traumatic ways but remember, stay strong and walk with the Lord, he will lead you through. Your third husband, that evaded you for a long time, (only emerging} once your children are grown with lives and children of their own}, will be a gem in comparison, and you will finally have the serenity in life that you had never know in any of your other relationships, family or otherwise.

At 27 years old you will break the band of child mode that you would unconsciously slip into around your mother, but fear not your humbleness, respect and adoration for your parents will reflect in the 6 children you will bring up single handily and you will relish in your reward and the Lord will bless you abundantly.

Fear not you have a great life in front of you so go forth and touch the world with a little of the blessings you have received from the hand of God, always remember him, always strive to live in his light and always, always be grateful and express your gratitude daily. This is your path to happiness so do not look back, go forward and embrace your life, there is much happiness to come. The world is your oyster, so live it to the fullest and look forward to the abundance of joy that is ahead for you.

Verona Ward
    Mother of 9 and grandmother to 30 (Truly blessed)

Know Your True Identity

Dear Anita,

Who am I? This is going to be a constant question that you are going to ask yourself; especially when you are being challenged, mentally and physically – but a challenge is good. Step into Gratitude whenever you feel that niggling feeling of doubt and depression. In fact, it is probably a sign that you are about to make a big breakthrough so keep persevering.

The world has given you some lessons that have shifted your direction dramatically but always remember you are always where you need to be at the right time. Losing your sight was a pivotal moment for you which has shaped you and driven you to achieve so much – it is in no way your identity, but it has shaped you. Chronic illness has given you a reason to strive for more and hold on to the precious moments of life, but again it's not your identity.

Being a single mother has shaken you to the core but again this is not your identity. Your current circumstances are not permanent and if you look within and sit with your heavenly father your next steps will be clear and in line with your identity.

Take a breath girl and pause, who do you need to prove to that you are Anita? God knows and loves you. Your identity should not be based on man's assumption of you. Your identity is important but girl does it really need defining constantly if you know who you are?

My biggest advice to you is focus on what's in front of you before moving onto the next thing this isn't to knock you but to just to ensure that you double check the finer details – your vision for the bigger picture is absolutely amazing but just be mindful if something is not in line with your identity or your life purpose leave it alone.

Close your eyes sister and keep on dreaming and enjoying your life, love you for you and embrace the challenges. Who am I? Girl you are the daughter of a king, a beautiful women of faith, an adventure seeker, a giver, an appreciator of life, passionate and compassionate. I could go on but I think you get the picture. Every single thing is possible, don't dwell on the past but grow and heal and leave all that does not serve you – you heard right leave all that does not serve you, I will say it again, leave all that does not serve you where it is.

Anita, I love you and want the best for you, stay focused and remember the vision you have for your life. Your identity has many layers and cannot be defined by one aspect of your life whether that be your disability, financial situation or singleness. Embrace it all and know that you are loved and focus on the vision you have for your life, it is always bigger than your current circumstances.

Love you and believe in you.

Anita Barzey
xxxxxx

What Is Your Why?

Dear Denise

Do you find it hard to answer the question "what is your why?" Whenever I use to hear that question, I shuddered. Emotionally shut down and excused the question as an esoteric quest for those struggling to find meaning in their life.

I realise that might seem arrogant. I've always known that I'm here to help others; to help them grow, challenge and change the status quo, to make a difference. But never took my answer any deeper than this until recently.....

You see, I've been working with a Business Coach and he had me working on this mighty question. I answered as I typically have, but with a bit more detail, thinking I nailed it! Until I received his feedback:

"You are doing great Denise!

I want you to dig deeper and push yourself harder. The tough part of being exceptional is that it's about your own personal improvement 1% more every day.

Go back and work on your Why. I want you to be able to make people want to hug you and be so happy they found you.

You did an awesome job and I am so proud of you for the effort. Now you have to make it even more clear, concise and compelling.

Work harder. The end product is you. Not a reflection of you, just you and you alone. You make the difference. You are the exception who can bring out the exceptional in others."

Denise? His feedback ignited something hidden deep within me, yearning to burst out. Without any thought, I wrote and wrote, holding nothing back. I share this with you now because it's our truth, our why, and the greatest gift I could ever give you.

"I lost my mom at age 8. I saw her for the first time in months the day before she died…

I should have known something was up! Days before this, relatives from all over the world, some of whom I'd never met, were here. I was so happy to see and have so many aunties, uncles and cousins all around me!

I remember being led into a semi lit hospital room. There she lay. And I couldn't believe it. My mom; she was frail, gaunt…small. That seemingly invincible powerhouse was reduced to a shell.

She called me over. My legs carried me towards her but I don't think I recall my feet hitting the ground. I grasped her hand; it was cold and weak.

She tried to talk to me, but the only thing I could make out was my name…her voice was a whisper, a speck of what I knew… but I responded as if I understood her.

Looking back, I do believe that on some level, that wordless soul level, I knew what she was trying to say: "don't be scared, be good, you're going to be ok…you're going to be and do great things Denise! And of course, I love you."

For so many years remembering that scene was one of sorrow and anguish. It was the end of hope; of her returning home and life as I knew it. I know firsthand no one on their deathbed wishes they worked more, made more money or had more things. They just want to be with the ones they love most and to tell them they mattered.

We had so many family & friends step up and care/support/guide us...I've never forgotten. I don't think I realised how profound their actions were, selfless; giving...it wasn't about pity. It was about love, and support, it was about giving selflessly, and community. All of them left a piece of themselves with me, and don't even know it.

I think of those people often and the roles they played in my life. I want to do that for others. To walk alongside them in their hour/time of need...to be their anchor, support, and more...pushing them forward...to live their purpose, their why. To help them live a life with no regrets for not living a life with greater meaning.

But in order to do that? I have to be the best version of me.

I want to be remembered for passing along the very best in me to others, so their lives are better, more fulfilled and happier in some way because I was part of it."

Denise? Don't shy away from these memories like I did. Embrace them. They empower you! Picture the good pieces of these moments, the feeling of mom looking over you, because she continues to champion you to this day! She knows you're strong and can and will do great things.

Know it's okay to be scared. Heck, who doesn't get scared from time to time?

Know that when you have the right people around you? You can move through fear and soar to your greatest. Your people, your champions, your tribe rallied around you back then. The same is true now. You have and will have more people championing you along your way Denise. Me being one of your BIGGEST champions!!

Embrace your why and go for whatever it is you want in life. It's all there for you. Leave no room for regrets, especially for not living a life Letters To My Younger Soul with greater meaning. When there is fulfilment and meaning to what we do, success just flows. It is us and is all around us.

Consider writing a letter to the people who helped you back then, sharing the impact they had on your life. Or, write pseudo letters, even in one letter, but don't send it to them. I think either of these (real letters or a pseudo letters) would be very cathartic to you.

Denise, we are always evolving. Today, you are your best version of you for the people you're meant to serve today. You're ready, you have everything in you; you simply need to believe this from the depth of your soul. Trust in you and Believe!

Denise Lorraine Aku Ledi

Real Change Starts Inside

Dear Deeqa

First off, stop obsessing over your current weight *spoiler* you are never going to be this 'heavy' again, EVER. I wonder sometimes what was so bad about our bodies, honestly. Social pressure does not help nor does the awkward navigation of being a teenager. There are so many things you are going through now and on top of all that, who decided that your body wasn't the RIGHT body?! The right TYPE of body because if I could combine Me now with You then we would be Invincible!!

As I sit here and write this, I think I may know where a lot of it came from, and the one word I can think of is shame, you are ashamed, I was ashamed WE were ashamed of our bodies. You were an early developer growing into your curves in your pre-teens not really catching up to what was happening. The mix of parental and cultural expectations that never allowed you to appreciate your self. In fact, made you doubt, feel closed up, hide away without dealing with the real issues of being able to accept yourself.

The weight was just one layer, you never thought you were enough, even losing the weight will not fix everything because you still can't look at yourself in the mirror naked and I know what else you're thinking who else would…

Wrong, wrong, wrong

The real change starts from the inside it was always on the inside and that sounds cliché, but it is the truth. You are so transfixed with losing weight but for who? It's not for yourself and as I mentioned before we're so transfixed with our size, reducing ourselves, our supposed 'BIG' size and yes, we are no longer that size... we are bigger! And that is ok.

The reason why I say its okay is that you...WE gain so much more then the numbers on the scale we gain confidence, appreciation and best of all a happier perspective of oneself.

Now I am not saying we wake up one day and all the self-hate disappears. It takes time...

We evolve and learn to let go and forgive ourselves. The key word is Forgiveness, and you would be surprised how long it took for me to come to that, it is forgiveness in not letting time do its thing, its forgiveness for never reaching a size and expectation that was never meant for us, and importantly forgiving what wrong we did to ourselves to move forward.

This probably sounds absurd because I would be thinking the same thing, how?! Trust me, we no longer inwardly cringe at what we see in the mirror instead we cannot wait to look, to check out that amazing women staring back at us.

The one who is healthy

thriving and

best of all, sound of mind because I am sure it gets so tiring putting yourself down, don't you think it's about time you pull us up?

All the best

Love Deeqa

Your Talents Will Shine

Dear Younger Self,

Body shaming is such a real problem in society, whether past, present or future. You might be teased for wearing braces, taunted over your glasses, ridiculed for not being thin enough or tall enough, or for being too thin and too tall. You'll meet people who despise curly hair and round face—who find problems with anything and everything. You need to know that their problem is not with you, but with their own insecurities and sense of self.

You're stronger than you think – physically, mentally and emotionally. Don't let others' perceptions of you weaken your own self esteem. People might tell you that you can't do many things — out of genuine concern or just to put you down — do it all anyways! You're smarter than they would have you believe. Your thoughts and opinions are valuable. You might not have people in your life now who believe and listen, but your well wishers are out there, and you will find your tribe someday.

Your talents will shine in time. The universe carries your energy and hopes, and brings positive wishes and light from people like you – the dreamers, the thinkers, the hopeful ones, and the ones who see beyond looking and listen beyond hearing. People are so much more than their outwardly figures, and it is important to look beyond the physical body, for others and yourself.

Pick up an instrument, learn a new language, take up a sport. There's no stopping the things you can do. Read, paint, draw, embroider, sing and write. Music and books do not care how you look. The author's story does not change and the piano or guitar won't play differently just because you're too short or too pale or have a ponytail that refuses to stay in place.

Your sense of rhythm makes you a great dancer, your love for the written word helps you find solace in reading and writing, knowing many languages expands your interactions with people and cultures from around the world, no matter what your body type might be. Long limbs make wonderful runners, but being short shouldn't stop you from running. Shorter limbs do well in weightlifting, but good muscle strength benefits tall people too. Frizzy hair doesn't dictate how well you can dance on stage. And flat feet do not decide your baking prowess or your skill with paper quilling.

Your creativity is a treasure, and imagination and talent have nothing to do with how you look. Do things you love to do without seeking validation from others. Forge good friendships, but find peace in solitude and be happy with your own company, too. True friends are the ones who stand the test of time. The most genuine are those who loved you when you didn't have anything, and didn't get envious when you had everything. Respect and trust can be more important than love. Your spirit is limitless, and the things you are capable of achieving have nothing to do with the way you look.

Renata Pavrey

Dearest, Rarest, Unusual Me

Dearest, rarest, unusual me.

Here conveys learned lessons linked to identity.

I urge you please, drink in the communication and context in which it's used.

Strip insecurity free from your person, completely nude. De-robe inferiority's niggle behind your giggle. Disengage fears doctrine through angelic insistent persistent assistance. Inhale truths light, savour OMNIPRESENT direction, ingest divine grammatical comprehension.

Exhale the panic chock-holding your gift and clamp onto purpose pure, walk through optimism's door. Wrangle NOT with distractions insignificant plot, to drain enthusiasm's aspiration from its slot. Rather resolve to zoom into what destiny presents you.
Yester-me spiritually discover, uncover, recover you.

Dearest, rarest, unusual me, our yesterday is riddled in ignorance's decay, funs due, wisdom's play, knowledge's clues and understanding's rays. I would greatly implore injections application brimming in diligence, fervour and chutzpah. Furthermore positivities keys and negativities boulder's will close in on your melanin wealthy, fluffy shoulders. Evading gravity, their both in a battle against life's sea

to sit and seize original identity. Future you applauds zeals welcome of all embedded in love, joy, generosity and mercy. Dispense your narrative liberally, our earth is ravenous for all creations manifestation. Excellence within churns out greatness once shared sparks contagiously fall and inflame the receptive.
Yester-me emotionally, discover, uncover, recover you

Dearest, rarest, unusual me,
Definitively, true identity requires observation's analysis.
One to one reflection, encompassing the exceptional, the atrocious, the exquisite, unseemly within the me genre. So younger, less certain yester-me I'd advise unfasten anxieties curtain.
Defrock societies conformity to imitate the majority.
Yester-me mentally discover, uncover, recover you

Dearest, rarest, unusual me, yesterday's rejections are intersections to boldly be addressed, adorned in perseverance eau de toilette. Remember your intrinsic and extrinsic armour, stand warrior queen, rise illuminated predestined ambassador. Allow the OMNIPOTENT lover of your soul governance, tutelage and council. Trust I AM'S plans, you're permanently engraved in HIS hand. Know that you know only in HIS infinite wisdom you'll grow.
Yester-me physically, discover, uncover, recover you.

Dearest, rarest, unusual me, yesterday's currency is spent, today's deposit rest in the reception of your faith. Identify your unique qualities, enter gratitudes gates, eat from humility's plate, complete discipline's race travel at consistencies pace grounding derailment's doubts into gravel. Tomorrow's credited by GRACE, so yester-me cleave to creations SOURCE, exit superficiallity's seduction wear love, give love, live love. Dance away from man's stereotypical conclusions of who you are, what you can, should, can't or shouldn't do. Yester-me just be the ULTIMATE, FORMIDABLE, IMMACULATE, INNOVATIVE, INVALUABLE MASTERPIECE GOD ALMIGHTY CREATED, FOREKNEW, CALLED, PREDESTINED, JUSTIFIED, GLORIFIED You to be.
YESTER-ME BE YOU, YESTER-ME BE YOU, YESTER-ME BE YOU.

Younger yester me / Younger yester you

Younger yester you, younger yester me be not entangled by what you lack
Intellectually, palpably, fervidly, intangibly

Younger yester me younger yester you
Atmosphere pays time no mention, nor gravity afford solar's heat it's attention
Permit yourself to be enthralled by LIFE'S TREE,
That worldly, inconsequential, corrupting debris
Fades from your impressionable lens

Younger yester you, younger yester me
Arise true in you
Leap not to man's juxtaposition erected collective
Root quintessence in gratefulness rather then materialisms vacuumed of placelessness
To covet what peers boast insatiably feeds appetites edacity audacious

Younger yester me younger yester you
Scarcely morph despondent as no's arrows are consistently prompted toward you
Like transparency ripples upon nile and dove's ascension in sky
Knock-backs are humilities adhesive cementing unrelenting appreciation for all encountered and accepted

Younger yester you, younger yester me
Restrain from feasting on capital credit
To falsify appearance for popularities adherence
Racking up debt, bent on breaking, shacking you from the bonding bliss
presented prior to birth

Younger yester me younger yester you
Live and let live, prevail entrenched in love,

Jump lights spectrum rope
Daily fermented within hope
Inherited by AUTHOR, NARRATOR, CREATOR

Younger yester you, younger yester me
As your soles correspond with earth
Allow a dalliance with compassions fortitude to
Enrapture, your heart, mind, and soul
Upon this juncture knowledge of discernments discretion permits you
intersession

Younger yester me, younger yester you
Settle your frame short, cute and sweet
Upon positions fellow soles may meet
Consume them not through miss-interpretation
Welcome them onto mantles constructed of illumination

Younger yester you, younger yester me
They've waded storms alien to you
You've vacationed nightmares many psyches dear not pursue
So in wonder of I AM one implore's
Younger yester me, younger yester you
Adopt a ravenous thirst for identities discovery
Walk adorned in royal robe
Head held high crowned foreknown
Predestined, called march
Justified, glorified on purpose soldier
Veering neither left nor right
Encased in armour trod on boldly
Younger yester you, younger yester me

Yester younger you, yester younger me

Yester younger me I know you fear the zone
Where nakedness stripes your comforts clothes
Embrace the fragments afraid, revel the thrill

Hammer away, nail it day by day pending peaceable fulfilment

Yester you conceal not what's real 'n' embedded
Press mute on peer comparisons
Stand up disregard shrinking to fit in
Sink inside contribution distinctively drawing you from seclusion

Yester younger me, be true in kindness
Plough difficulties maze enriched, by resource
A soul orphaned of council wanders off it's course

Yester younger me discord intrinsic to essence caused through fright
Bites away light established to thee
Though a child settling in whales 'n' wallows for guardian
Solace governed by interest allows acceptance to follow
It's like the quote by Dr.King "take the first step, the whole staircase
doesn't have to be seen"

Yester younger you there's nothing to prove
To any shade of male / female hue
But you've everything to lose in in-action
Stagnancy not divinely decreed breeds procrastinations panic, anxieties
inadequacies, and depressions instability.

Yester younger me though your dreams terrify seemingly
insurmountable
Rise girl rise the power inside undoubtable and
Though by social perception innumerable
As you believe upon the WAY, receive from the TRUTH
You'll achieve by way of LIFE

Yester younger you some seasons you plant and some you reap
With GOD child all things in alignment with HIS WILL are made
possible that you seek
Steer clear of temptations jaw, enticingly sweet
However at leisurely pace evicts you from honors stable place

Convicting till you're sitting listing regrets, your joys engulfed by stress
Raising the roof in your duress
Yester younger me unlatch you're popularity clutching

Trend train zombie longing, not your taste, yet you'll waste space in time energy on belonging
Yester younger you ease don't seize up, soften, live, laugh, savour nature
Valleys seminars, mountain peaks grandeur

Yester younger me battles of discussion and repercussion through assumptions lens
Yester younger you speak your mind under respectful tone, in love at times, in contexts and locations directed from above.

Anointed Sonnet

Afterword

The search for the women to take part in this book began with a call to friends and family, then associates and colleagues. What was embraced with vigour and fervour in the first instance by all, soon became a quest for the brave, the uninhibited, the fearless and those who were tired of hiding.

This is not to say anyone who didn't participate is not worthy of such attributes, but it soon become clear that this was and is a cathartic journey we should all take more than perhaps we realise or desire to.

Armed with the instruction of writing to a particular topic, such as Mental Health, Sex, Parents, and Careers, letters were penned and submitted in the hope that they would make the grade. All were more than we expected.

It was also clear that for most, if not all, their chosen focus was a matter they had processed. Something they had sought to understand and had grown to be somewhat at peace with.

So, I want to encourage every women, no matter the age, that reads these letters to take their own journey of letter writing. Not to have it published in a book necessarily, but to begin a journey of recovery, restoration, rejuvenation, redemption, reconciliation, resolution and relief.

As the project progressed, it became apparent that many of us carry deep wounds, deep hurts and injustices that we don't brag about, we don't share and that can simply take on the form of the old adage of being the 'small foxes that spoil the vine.' They become those things that are never big enough to grind your life to a halt, but enough to cause you to choose options that go against your better judgment, if you don't tend to them.

Start writing now. It's better out than in, as the saying goes. You may throw away the first one; you may throw away the next 10. You may start today and not finish for a month, but start you should.

It's unlikely to change over night. There will be little noticeable change at first just by changing direction, or doing something different. However, there is a school of thought that says if you change by one percent each day for one year, by the end of it you will end up thirty-seven times better.

Every journey starts with one step, and a one percent change is small enough to almost seem insignificant, but it's the accumulative effect that matters, so begin; one thought, one word, one sentence, one letter at a time.

Maureen
xx

Printed in Great Britain
by Amazon

70339238R00095